How to Get a Management NVQ, Level 4

Book 1: Mandatory Units

How to Get a Management NVQ, Level 4

Book 1: Mandatory Units

Richard Johnson and Cathy Parker

Letts Educational
Aldine Place
LONDON
W12 8AW
Tel: 0181-740 2268
Fax: 0181-743 8451
e-mail: he@lettsed.co.uk

Acknowledgements

We would like to begin by acknowledging all those candidates who have helped develop the concept for this book, as it was their need for a supporting text that was the driving force behind its development. In addition, the content of the book has evolved through supporting candidates through various stages of their qualification. We are indebted to those people who have allowed us to refine our methods and advice over the past four years. Special thanks should go to Heather Muir and Alan Follett for their support, ideas and discussion, and to Donna for her typing skills. We are sure that we will continue to learn from the experiences and efforts of others, and would therefore encourage readers of our book to contact us (FreshThink@aol.com) with their comments and feedback.

Essex County Council Libraries

A CIP catalogue record for this book can be obtained from the British Library

ISBN 1-85805-346-3

Copyright Richard Johnson and Cathy Parker © 1998

The National Occupational Standards for Management were developed by the MCI with DfEE funding. This material is Crown copyright and is reproduced under licence from the Controller of Her Majesty's Stationery Office.

Designed and typeset by Ian Foulis & Associates, Plymouth, Devon

Printed and bound in Great Britain by Ashford Colour Press, Gosport, Hants

Contents

Preface

How to Get a Management NVQ has been developed as a direct result of our involvement in management development programmes across a number of industries and sectors, from social services to mining and everything in between.

Challenged with the task of supporting managers in their quest to achieve their Management NVQ, a major issue confronted us: the realities of work-based learning. What were Management NVQ candidates to do when they could not get access to advice? Our research suggests that although the majority of managers collect the evidence for their NVQ at work, the amount of peace and tranquillity they need in order to reflect and write up their analysis is unlikely to be found in a busy office, with 101 things still on the 'to do' list. Calmer surroundings are usually found at home, often after the children/partner/dog/cat have settled for the evening, at which time so too has the manager's NVQ advisor. So the need for supportive materials became apparent. Managers live and work in the oddest of places – they cannot always get to centralised seminars, workshops and classes held at their local college, TEC or training centre. *How to Get a Management NVQ* seeks to address these issues – to give you your own portable advisor that never sleeps and that aims to support you during the process of obtaining a Management NVQ.

To get your Management NVQ you will need to identify, analyse and reference hard evidence of your competence as a manager; *How to Get a Management NVQ* simply assists you in this process. Unit by unit, chapters help you to interpret the standards required by the qualification and make them meaningful and relevant to *your* job in *your* workplace. Each page has an area set aside for note making, evidence identification and even labelling for future reference. Relevant questions are asked, suggestions for areas of reflection and analysis are made, and recommendations for items of hard evidence are also included.

Anyone alarmed by the amount of jargon associated with NVQs will be pleased to learn that the book is written in plain English. NVQ jargon is explained and the portfolio-building process examined and illustrated. *How to Get a Management NVQ* will confirm and reassure your thoughts and reflections, supporting your ideas and actions. It will also drive you towards identifying new areas of work and evidence for inclusion in your NVQ. In contrast to generic texts, this series gets to the heart of the practical aspects of undertaking a Management NVQ and will assist you to achieve the qualification without compromising your approach. Enjoy the process!

Richard Johnson and Cathy Parker

Introduction

> 'To realise our ambition, we must all develop and sustain a regard for learning at whatever age. For many people this will mean overcoming past experiences which have put them off learning. For others it will mean taking the opportunity, perhaps for the first time, to recognise their own talent, to discover new ways of learning and to see new opportunities opening up.'
>
> David Blunkett, Secretary of State for Education and Employment, 'The Learning Age', 1988

Background

This book has been conceived and published during an exciting time for learning and development. The new Labour government has announced its commitment to 'lifelong learning', major companies refer to themselves as 'learning organisations', and academics and practitioners in the field announce the arrival of 'the learning century' (Longworth and Davies, 1996). Obviously, those responsible for the nation's education and training appear to have welcomed these ideas. But what do all these concepts and labels mean to *learners* themselves? In terms of alterations to 'the learning system', the outcomes of change are apparent. New forms of qualification, such as NVQs, are rivalling traditional ones, and new ways of learning, far different to the ones most of us grew up with, are being championed. NVQs are vocational qualifications that rely on a myriad of approaches to learning and development, designed to meet the needs of industry and the individual rather than those of the educational providers. In a review of 100 NVQs and SVQs carried out by Gordon Beaumont (1997), the benefits of adopting NVQs were seen to outweigh the costs by 77 per cent of users. Nevertheless, despite the interest in and commitment to the concepts of lifelong learning and the integration of the term 'NVQ' into our everyday vocabulary, much confusion surrounds these topics.

Who is this book for?

This book has been written to support any candidate (or potential candidate) working with the revised MCI management standards at Level 4 (which were launched in January 1998). The book focuses on the five *mandatory* units of the qualification. As NVQs are a relatively new form of qualification, many candidates feel in the dark when it comes to actually doing one. Those in search of help and support cannot always access it, for a variety of reasons. Because of the demand for the qualification, many organisations and individuals have found themselves in the role of provider, sometimes with little experience or training. Another issue is the nature of the qualification itself. It is a work-based qualification to be completed, primarily, in the workplace. This means that those studying for it cannot rely on traditional means of support (weekly classes, fellow students, etc.).

What does it do?

As a result of being involved with Management NVQs over the past five years, we have realised that although every portfolio put forward for assessment is different, the process each candidate goes through, the problems they face and the questions they ask, are all very similar. It is these issues that we address in this book. By working through its contents, you will understand the requirements of the mandatory units of the qualification and avoid replicating some of the mistakes of those who have gone through the process before you. No book can or should replace a good advisor, but by using both sources of support you can ensure that you make the best possible use of your time with her or him.

Structure

The book is divided into two parts. The first part of the book explains the background to and nature of the qualification so that you can understand why you are studying for it. This section looks at the practicalities of progressing your NVQ by explaining the process of portfolio building and also introduces the other people who will be important to you as you progress your NVQ – people such as your advisor and assessor. Most importantly, this section also tells you about the level of service you can reasonably expect from these people, information that we hope will help to raise the standard and recognition of the qualification to the level it deserves. The second part of the book concentrates on actually *doing* your NVQ. By working through each chapter, using the prompts provided, you will soon find that you have a portfolio of evidence ready for assessment. We have also included the experiences of four real-life candidates so that you can see that you are not alone in your experiences.

Part One An Introduction to Management NVQs

The first part of this book explains what a Management NVQ is, the background to the qualification, the people involved, and how to build a portfolio of evidence. You may need to refer to the glossary (page 314) to get the most out of this section. If you are new to the NVQ process we recommend that you read this section fully. If you are familiar with this type of qualification, you may still find that it contains some useful information.

Part One An Introduction to Management NVQs

CHAPTER 1

What is a Management NVQ?

The first question any candidate registered for a Management NVQ asks is: 'What is a Management NVQ?' This chapter aims to answer this question. We do this first by establishing the background to Management NVQs, to enable you to understand the growth of the NVQ movement. Next we define and explain the nature of the qualification itself, so that you understand exactly what you are striving to achieve. We compare the award to other, more traditional qualifications to help you understand the level of the qualification for which you are studying. Finally, we summarise the process of achieving the qualification, so that you have a realistic idea of the amount of time and work involved in gaining a Management NVQ at Level 4.

Background

Vocational education and training in management has received central government support from its inception. Two government reports – *The Making of British Managers* (Constable and McCormick, 1987) and *The Making of Managers* (Handy, Gow and Moloney, 1987) – identified the need for competence-based education and training. This need coincided with the establishment of the National Council for Vocational Qualifications (NCVQ) and the Scottish Qualifications Authority (SQA) in 1980. NCVQ is now the Qualifications and Curriculum Authority (QCA) and it oversees all 896[1] NVQs, including all six Management NVQs. The Management NVQs were first introduced in 1991. They were developed by the Management Charter Initiative (MCI), which was set up to form a link between government, industry and education in order to develop the Management NVQs and to foster and sustain long-term commitment to their success. This commitment has continued to the present, with the Labour government signalling its intention to support the continued adoption of NVQs across all industries. Over 1,600,000 NVQs have now been awarded.

As an NVQ candidate, you are certainly not alone, but what accounts for this level of interest in Management NVQ programmes? It can be traced back to two economic reports of the 1980s, commissioned by the government. Both the Handy Report (Confederation of British Industry) and the McCormick Report (National Economic Development Office) supported the NVQ movement through their examination of management development and education in the UK.

---

[1] This figure represents all NVQs at all levels (compiled from *DataNews*, Winter 1997/98).

Their conclusions were as follows:

- Management training is a key factor in economic growth.

- UK managers receive little or no training.

- Existing management training provision was too small for such a vast labour pool.

- Existing provision was too eclectic; formats need to be standardised and nationally recognised across industries.

- Any new framework should place emphasis on job training and personal development.

Of course, the success of NVQs is not wholly dependent on the support of government. To become a viable alternative to other forms of management development, NVQs needed to appeal to employers. NVQs represent an economic alternative to traditional training methods because the costs incurred in terms of staff replacement and related expenses are considerably lower than those associated with traditional qualifications. This is because development occurs on the job and is directly relevant to the manager's performance. This can be compared to classroom-based methods of training, which are often not directly relevant to the manager's job and take place outside the workplace.

Finally, there are the candidates themselves. The qualification has to be relevant to their needs, as they are the ones who actually have to make the effort to get it. Because of the changing nature of work, employees find themselves under increasing pressure. A number of factors contribute to this; for instance, downsizing means that, in many organisations, there are fewer employees left to do the same (or sometimes more) work. This puts pressure on those who want to attend day-release courses to obtain a qualification. Because of the harsh economic conditions facing many organisations, funding for this type of development has often been severely reduced. Anecdotal evidence from candidates also suggests that managers (especially those with families) are increasingly reluctant to give up evenings and weekends to attend courses. Nevertheless, because of growing uncertainty among many in employment (fuelled by the rising number of temporary contracts, endless calls for early retirement, rounds of redundancies, etc.), managers need qualifications that reflect their skills and experience. It is hardly surprising that a qualification as flexible as an NVQ, which can be undertaken at times convenient for the candidate, is proving so popular among employees concerned about the content of their curriculum vitae.

Definition of NVQs

A National Vocational Qualification is defined as

> 'a statement of competence relevant to employment. It is this statement which specifies the competence to be achieved. It is the basis from which assessment procedures and recording and certification can be derived'

> (NCVQ, 1988)

The key part of this definition is the issue of competence. The Training Agency (1989) has defined competence as the ability to:

◼ Perform whole work roles (perform – not just know about – the whole job rather than just specific skills and tasks).

◼ Perform to the standards expected in employment (not just 'training' standards or standards divorced from industrial reality).

◼ Perform in real working environments (with all the associated pressures and variations of real work).

An NVQ prescribes standards of competence that have to be met and consolidates these standards into a formal qualification. NVQs are based on explicit standards of competence, which are written down for everybody to see, in a standardised and nationally recognised format. NVQ statements of competence are identified from an analysis not of educational and training programmes but of employment requirements. The analysis is carried out by, or on behalf of, employers and employees in the relevant sector, and the final product (i.e. the NVQ) has to be endorsed by them and approved by the QCA before it can be offered to candidates. The MCI carried out this function for the Management NVQs; they developed the standards and are therefore termed the lead body, which means that they are responsible for the upkeep of the standards. In the past, this has meant rewriting them to ensure that they continue to be relevant to the needs of industry. By having nationally agreed standards of competence laid down for managers, any manager who can demonstrate that she or he meets these standards is, by definition, competent. For the first time, competent managers have an opportunity to prove it.

Content

All NVQs can be broken down into a number of constituent parts (Figure 1):

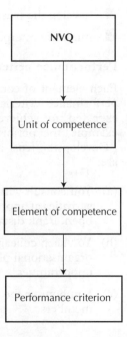

Figure 1
An illustration of the constituent parts of all NVQs

Units of competence

Units of competence refer to key aspects of management. For example, there are six core units in the Management NVQ at Level 4. These are:

- Unit A2 – Manage activities to meet requirements
- Unit A4 – Contribute to improvements at work
- Unit C2 – Develop your own resources
- Unit C5 – Develop productive working relationships
- Unit D4 – Provide information to support decision making

And one of either Unit B2 or B3

- Unit B2 – Manage the use of physical resources
- Unit B3 – Manage the use of financial resources

As you can see, a unit neatly encapsulates an area of management, for instance Unit C5 is concerned with people management. In addition to these six units, you have to pick three optional units from a choice of 18. It is important that the optional units you pick reflect the job you do, otherwise you will not be able to generate or collect suitable evidence. Before you decide on your choice of optional units, you should talk to your advisor.

Elements of competence

Within each unit of competence there are elements of competence. These broadly reflect what managers are expected to do within each area (or unit) of management. Within Unit C5 ('Develop productive working relationships'), the elements require proof that you:

- develop the trust and support of colleagues and team members (Element C5.1);
- develop the trust and support of your manager (Element C5.2);
- minimise interpersonal conflict (Element C5.3).

Performance criteria

Each element of competence is made up of a series of very specific performance criteria. These describe in detail what a manager is expected to achieve in order to demonstrate competence. For example, the performance criteria associated with Element C5.1 ('Develop the trust and support of colleagues and team members') are:

(a) You consult with colleagues and team members about proposed activities at appropriate times and in a manner which encourages open, frank discussion.

(b) You keep colleagues and team members informed about organisational plans and activities, emerging threats and opportunities.

(c) You honour the commitments you make to colleagues and team members.

(d) You treat colleagues and team members in a manner which shows your respect for individuals and the need for confidentiality.

(e) You give colleagues and team members sufficient support for them to achieve their work objectives.

(f) You discuss discreetly with the colleagues and team members concerned your evaluation of their work and behaviour.

Level

A Level 4 NVQ is defined as:

> 'Competence which involves the application of knowledge in a broad range of complex, technical or professional work activities performed in a wide variety of contexts and with a substantial degree of personal responsibility and autonomy. Responsibility for the work of others and the allocation of resources is often present.'

> Qualifications and Curriculum Authority (QCA), 1998

We have already established that competence-based qualifications focus on developing a candidate's work activities in line with nationally recognised standards. Because of this, competence-based qualifications differ considerably from academic qualifications, although comparisons between the two have been made. For example, a Level 3 MCI qualification in management (NVQ3) has been considered to be the equivalent of a National Diploma in a similar subject. Similarly, Level 4 MCI qualifications (NVQ4) have been equated with higher qualifications such as the Diploma in Management Studies (DMS). However, as competence-based qualifications have become more common in the workplace, it is apparent that comparisons of this kind are misleading since the nature and purpose of the two types of qualification are so different. In general, academic qualifications tend to focus on theoretical scenarios or the application of theory to a work situation. In contrast, competence-based qualifications focus on what candidates are already doing in their jobs and seek to develop their individual skills in the workplace.

Getting the award

In this section, we explain the process of obtaining a Management NVQ. Figure 2 on page 10 represents the process as a diagram.

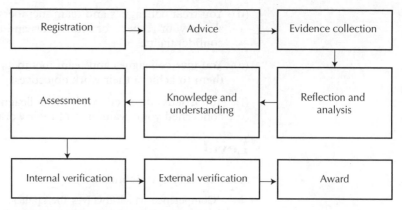

Figure 2
The process of obtaining
an NVQ

Registration

The first stage of your NVQ will be registration with an awarding body. Currently, there are 16 organisations that are allowed to award a Management NVQ at Level 4; these are:

- City and Guilds
- Edexcel (formally BTEC)
- Engineering and Marine Training Authority
- Henley Management College
- Institute for Supervision and Management
- Institute of Personnel and Development
- London Chamber of Commerce and Ind. Examinations Board
- Management Verification Consortium
- RSA Examinations Board
- The College of Preceptors
- The Institute of Management
- The Institute of the Motor Industry
- The Institute of Operations Management
- The National Examining Board for Supervision and Management (NEBSM)
- The Open University
- University of Oxford Delegacy of Local Examinations

In terms of the management standards it makes no difference which awarding body you register with, since by their nature national standards do not change across providers. The only difference between awarding bodies is their interpretation of how certain aspects of the NVQ process should be managed. In this book we adopt a rigorous approach that will ensure you meet the requirements of the most demanding of awarding bodies.

You will register with your awarding body through an assessment centre. Assessment centres are organisations (or parts of organisations) that have been granted the opportunity to offer an awarding body's NVQ. In your case, your assessment centre could be:

- your own organisation;
- a local college/university;
- a private training provider;
- a professional body (e.g. The Institute of Management).

Often, two or more of these organisations work together to provide you with your NVQ. For example, within Durham County Council Social Services management candidates are registered with NEBSM (the awarding body) through East Durham Community College. However, the support services required by candidates (for example, advice and assessment) are provided by a combination of in-house staff and outside private training providers. Nevertheless, the responsibility for the standard of service all these people provide ultimately rests with the assessment centre. In the case of Durham County Council, this is now the responsibility of their Staff Development Section, as they have recently been awarded assessment centre status from NEBSM.

From your perspective, one of the most important outcomes of registering is being given the management standards themselves. These are the standards of competence that you will have to demonstrate in order to be awarded your NVQ.

Advice

Once you have registered for your award, you should soon be allocated an advisor, who will help you achieve the requirements of the qualification. We detail what you can expect from your advisor in chapter 2. In this section we'll concentrate on where advice fits into the NVQ process. If you are one of a number of people studying for the same award, you may find that your early NVQ advice takes place within a workshop setting, where standard information can be more efficiently transmitted to a number of people. Typically, these workshops will cover much of the content we are focusing on in part one of this book. In other words, they serve as an introduction to the NVQ process. Some providers continue this workshop approach throughout the qualification. However, a good provider will offer these in addition to one-to-one advice.

The first one-to-one session or *initial audit* you are likely to have with your advisor will probably focus on understanding exactly what you do and what you have done in the past. The proper terminology for this is Accredited Prior Learning/Achievement (APL/A). In other words, your advisor will want to know if there is anything that you can put forward in order to save you unnecessary work. For example, if you already have a formal business qualification (such as an HNC in Business and Finance), it would be pointless to have to prove again your knowledge and understanding of the theoretical issues you have already covered in your HNC. In this case your qualification (the HNC) would be evidenced as Accredited Prior Learning. Of course, you would have to provide hard evidence of this. For example, you could include the certificate of award and the syllabus in your portfolio of evidence. You would also link this evidence back to the NVQ. For example, you could link the relevant syllabus items to specific requirements of the NVQ. As you progress your NVQ, your advisor will help you understand and interpret the standards, give you ideas for evidence, and often undertake mock assessments of your work before it is actually submitted for assessment.

Evidence collection

The idea behind the achievement of an NVQ is extraordinarily simple. A standard of competence is laid down (by the MCI) and you have to find some evidence to prove that you meet that standard. For example, one of the standards (performance criterion, to give it its proper name) requires you to '*assess your performance and identify your development needs at appropriate intervals*'. So, how could you prove that you actually did this in the workplace? One way might be to include documentation relating to any self-appraisal activities you carried out in the workplace. Or perhaps you discuss this type of thing with your manager or mentor during appraisal meetings. It will be up to you (with the help of your advisor) to decide what evidence will prove the requirements of the standard. A huge part of your NVQ will involve collecting evidence for your portfolio. We cover the types of evidence you can collect in more detail in chapter 3. As you get the hang of doing your NVQ, you will start to think more about evidence collection as part of your daily routine. For example, one candidate started to write more details about forthcoming meetings in her diary so that these diary pages could be photocopied and used as evidence. As a result, she found that she was more prepared for meetings as she always knew what they were going to be about!

Reflection and analysis

Getting an NVQ is not merely a case of putting pieces of paper in a portfolio. Whatever evidence you submit in support of the management standards in which you are trying to prove competence must be explained. Your *reflection* upon and *analysis* of your evidence in terms of the management standards demonstrates to your assessor that you understand how you meet the requirements of the qualification. As assessors, we know how frustrating it is when candidates submit evidence in a portfolio with little or no attempt to explain why it is relevant. Remember, your assessor is there to help you, but she/he is not (always) telepathic! Reflection and analysis also gives you the opportunity to demonstrate your underlying knowledge and understanding of the related issues deemed important by the Management NVQ. You complete your reflection and analysis on stationery provided by your training provider/assessment centre. There is a completed example of this in Appendix 1.

Knowledge and understanding

An NVQ is not just about proving your competence through evidence gathered in the workplace. In addition to this, you need to prove that you understand why you do what you do. In other words, you will need to demonstrate that your actions at work are underpinned by your knowledge of relevant theories/principles/methods/models, etc. The way in which you meet the knowledge part of your NVQ may vary, depending on your provider. Some providers test knowledge through the use of formal tests and questions. Others prefer to set assignments that cover the requirements of the qualification. In some cases, knowledge and understanding may be linked to another course whose content meets some or all of the requirements of the NVQ.

For example, you may have already studied for a business qualification and this achievement could be evidenced as Accredited Prior Learning (APL). A few providers (especially colleges and universities) have integrated NVQs into their existing academic provision. These providers are, in effect, offering a joint award: a certificate that credits the knowledge and understanding of the candidate, and an NVQ that credits their competence in the workplace. Finally, your reflection and analysis can be used to demonstrate your underpinning knowledge and understanding. In our experience, it is advisable to make use of all these methods – choosing the most appropriate one for each situation as it arises.

Assessment

Assessment is the process whereby the evidence in your portfolio is compared with the NVQ standards in order to determine whether or not you are competent. This is a formal process and should not be confused with any general advice, feedback and support your assessor may give you during the development of your portfolio. When your portfolio is returned following assessment, you will find that the assessor has made a written copy of her/his assessment decision. There are three possible assessment decisions:

- Competent
- Not yet competent
- Insufficient evidence

If a candidate is not credited 'competent', the most likely assessment decision she or he will receive is that of insufficient evidence. In other words, a candidate may well be competent in an area of her or his job, but the evidence presented does not confirm this. Remember, your assessor is often external to your organisation and so what is obvious to you may not be so to her or him. Use your reflection and analysis sheets to explain *why* your evidence meets the requirements of the standard.

Internal verification

One of the main challenges to the success of NVQs is ensuring that levels of quality are maintained. For the first time, many organisations outside the education sector are involved in supporting those who are working towards a national qualification. For instance, you may well find that your own advisor or assessor is also a work colleague, who has received training in this role. One of the ways in which the quality of the system can be assured is through the process of verification. The first level of verification is internal verification. This is carried out by an internal verifier, who is attached to your assessment centre. The internal verifier randomly samples portfolios in order to ensure that standards are being maintained. She or he is looking to see that assessment decisions are comparable:

- across candidates
- across assessors
- across units

The internal verifier is not there to catch out the assessor – in fact, she or he has no power to overturn assessment decisions – but is there to check the quality of the whole programme. We look at their role in more depth in chapter 2.

External verification

The system for external verification is similar to that for internal verification. The external verifier is attached not to your assessment centre but to the awarding body with which you are registered. Again, the external verifier randomly samples portfolios in order to ensure standards are being maintained. She or he is looking to see that the NVQs awarded are comparable:

- across candidates
- across assessors
- across programmes

Again, the external verifier is more interested in the quality of the whole programme in relation to other programmes than in individual cases. For more information on the role of the external verifier see chapter 2.

Award

Finally, when you have been deemed competent in every unit and your portfolio has been internally and externally verified, your assessment centre will apply to the awarding body for your award.

Time

Because of the flexible nature of the qualification, predicting how long it will take is obviously not an exact science. From our experience with candidates, each unit can reasonably be expected to take about six weeks. So, a candidate could complete a Management NVQ (at Level 4) in 13.5 months (nine units x 1.5 months). Two factors affect the time it takes a candidate to complete a unit. First, candidates differ as to their speed of completion. This can be due to a number of factors, the most common (in our experience) being pressures at work and the level of motivation to complete the qualification. Although the qualification is flexible in terms of time, a registered candidate has to complete within 36 months of registering, although this varies between awarding bodies.

Another factor is the turnaround time of assessment. Candidates (particularly during the early stages of their NVQ) do not like to start a new unit before they have had feedback from the last one they submitted. A good assessment centre will have a reasonable turnaround time for assessment (for example, two weeks). Unfortunately, some candidates have to wait a lot longer and this obviously affects how long it takes them to complete the qualification. Once completed, your NVQ still has to be verified, and as the external verifier is responsible for many assessment centres, this is often not particularly instant. Once your NVQ has been verified, the awarding body has to generate the relevant paperwork, including your certificate, and the time it takes for this can vary widely across awarding bodies. As a very general guide, as long as you are sufficiently self-motivated and have an efficient assessment centre and awarding body, you can expect to be receiving your NVQ certificate about 18 months after registering for your award.

CHAPTER 2

People involved in your NVQ

There are two reasons why we included this chapter. First, we wanted candidates to be clear about the people who would be involved in their NVQ. We have therefore used this chapter to explain who they are and what they do. Our second reason is to assist in raising the quality of NVQ provision. This chapter explains what your rights are with regard to those who support you. If you feel you are not getting the service to which you are entitled, this chapter also describes the options that are open to you.

Advisor

Your advisor will be the most important source of help and advice when it comes to progressing your NVQ. Many organisations now run their NVQ programmes in-house, which means that your advisor may well be a fellow employee. All advisors should be qualified to accredit prior learning (this means that they should already have their Training and Development Lead Body (TDLB) NVQ Unit D36), as this will be one of the roles they perform. In addition to this, your advisor should be *occupationally competent* in your work area. You can expect your advisor to guide you throughout the whole NVQ process. Don't be afraid to ask advice – that's what your advisor is there for! In particular, your advisor will help you find evidence of any prior learning or achievement that will be relevant to your NVQ. She or he will help you understand the standards and interpret them in ways relevant to your work. When it comes to identifying suitable evidence, your advisor can help you ensure that the evidence you select meets the requirements of the qualification. Should your assessor decide you are 'not yet competent' in any area, your advisor can help you understand the feedback and make the necessary alterations to your portfolio.

You may find yourself in the position of not meeting a specific performance criterion simply because your work role does not cover that area. In this case your advisor can offer you opportunities to gather the necessary evidence through simulation if, in relation to the management standards, this is a viable alternative. Finally, your advisor may offer you ways of demonstrating your knowledge and understanding through, for example, assignments or written tests.

Assessor

Again, as many NVQ programmes are run in-house, your assessor could well be a work colleague. Regardless of whether your assessor is internal or external to your organisation, she or he should be qualified to undertake assessment decisions (by having achieved

TDLB NVQ Units D32 and D33), be occupationally competent in your work area and understand the organisation within which you work. Your assessor should assist you and your advisor in drawing up an assessment plan. It may be that, for some evidence, your assessor will have to observe you on the job and this means arranging mutually convenient times. You should expect your assessor to return your portfolio within a mutually agreed time limit. In addition, you should also expect that any assessment decision is supported by thorough feedback. Finally, you have the right to expect your assessor to complete all the relevant documentation regarding the assessment process.

Internal verifier

Your internal verifier will be attached to your assessment centre and should hold TDLB NVQ Unit D34. Your internal verifier plays an important role in quality assurance, as she or he ensures that the assessment decisions are accurate. You may not meet your internal verifier, but, over the course of your NVQ, your portfolio certainly will.

External verifier

Your external verifier is attached to your awarding body and should possess TDLB NVQ Unit D35. You should endeavour to meet your external verifier, if possible, as she or he may be able to offer valuable advice in terms of what is happening in other organisations. Again, the external verifier's role is one of quality assurance, monitoring the output of assessment centres.

Work colleagues

If you are going through the NVQ process with colleagues at work, you will find yourself at a considerable advantage over those who have to go it alone. In our experience, those candidates who have formed 'buddy groups' have progressed their NVQ more efficiently than those working independently. Informal meetings with colleagues will allow you to share information and ideas. You can learn from the experiences of others and, in return, they can learn from yours. Finally, discussing your NVQ with others has several organisational benefits. For example, you may find that issues you thought were unique to you are, in fact, far more widespread and may therefore require some organisational intervention. In one company, candidates came together to discuss the issue of appraisal, since they had to prove they underwent regular appraisal to meet the requirements of the NVQ. In the absence of a company appraisal system, the candidates between them developed their own and presented it to their senior managers, who approved of the idea and decided to implement it, after minor adaptation.

Assessment centre

Your assessment centre has been awarded the right to administer your NVQ programme on behalf of an awarding body. You should expect your assessment centre to have appropriate resources to do this. For example, it will need to have a suitable management information system that can record and store all the information required by the awarding body and other interested parties, such as funding councils. It will also need systems in place to monitor and ensure the quality of assessment decisions. It should also promote equal and open access to assessment and have suitably competent staff to undertake and verify assessment decisions.

Complaints and appeals

If you are concerned about an assessment decision, your first port of call should be the assessor who made the assessment decision. In our experience, the majority of concerns, when discussed between candidate and assessor, are rectified. However, if the concern cannot be resolved, you should then contact your advisor or assessment centre. Your assessment centre should publish its complaints and appeals procedure. Once you have this, you can ensure that your complaint is dealt with. If your concern is about another aspect of your NVQ, you will need to contact whoever is in charge of your programme.

CHAPTER 3

Building your NVQ portfolio

In this chapter we look more closely at how you will achieve your Management NVQ. Your whole qualification will be based on your portfolio of evidence. This will take the form of one or more files which will contain all the evidence you compile over the coming months. This chapter also explains the type of evidence you will be putting into your portfolio. For a full explanation of the types of evidence referred to here that are unique to the NVQ process, consult the glossary.

What is a portfolio of evidence?

This is your own personal collection of evidence that proves that your performance meets the standards of the NVQ. It is likely to take the form of one or more lever arch or ring binder files.

Evidence

The content of your portfolio, put forward in support of the management standards you are attempting to meet, is termed evidence. Evidence should be gathered over the coming months and should correspond with the requirements of each unit, element and performance criterion (PC) of the Management NVQ. You use the evidence you submit to prove your competence. Evidence can take a variety of different forms. We have compiled the following analysis of evidence from our experience with candidates over the past four years.

Types of evidence

Evidence can be classified in two ways: performance evidence and supplementary evidence.

Performance evidence

Whenever possible, you should attempt to produce evidence based on naturally occurring (routine) work activities. The evidence you generate as a result of performing your normal work role is termed performance evidence. It is hard proof of your competence as a manager. Depending on the nature of the evidence, it can be recorded through observation by an advisor or assessor, audio or video recordings, observations by colleagues, subordinates, managers or service users/customers. Here are some examples of performance evidence that candidates have used.

- Reports
- Memos
- Minutes of meetings
- Records of activities
- Notes of action
- Records of projects
- Staff/business objectives
- Business plans
- Contracts
- Budgets
- Quotations
- Purchasing documentation
- Advertising
- Letters
- Job descriptions
- Personnel specifications
- Training plans
- Personal/staff development plans
- Video/audio recordings of your performance
- Induction materials
- Appraisal reports
- References
- Testimonies
- Training evaluation
- Diary/log sheets
- Photographs
- Assessor's written observational analysis sheet (see below)

All the evidence listed above is described as naturally occurring evidence. In other words, it is a by-product of the job you do. Including this evidence in your portfolio would be a matter of photocopying something that already existed or recording a conversation you were going to have anyway. In some cases, it is not practical to include certain evidence in your portfolio. For example, if you are dealing with confidential information, you may not want this information to leave the building. In these cases, your assessor could visit you at work in order to make the assessment decision on the spot. Your assessor would provide you with evidence of this in the form of an observational analysis sheet.

Event route
One important category of performance evidence is that of the event route. This refers to one whole process or activity which a candidate

uses to meet a large chunk of her or his NVQ requirement. The event route focuses on specific areas of your responsibility. It allows you to demonstrate competence against the national standards in a constructive and logical way. Rather than taking a pick-and-mix approach to evidence, the event route allows you to take a specific body of your work and match it against the requirements of the NVQ.

The benefits of taking the event route

The event route allows you to examine and review your job role in detail. It will focus you on the stages of a process or project and assist you in maximising the evidence available. It will also provide a logical sequence of evidence that makes sense to you and can be clearly understood by your assessor and the verifiers involved.

How do I take the event route?

You will need to identify definable areas of your work and then match them against the units of competence that you are undertaking. These areas could include *events* such as special projects, functional processes or certain procedures for which you are responsible. For example:

Special projects:

- your remit
- the other people involved and their responsibility
- the resources available
- timescales
- allocation of tasks
- the work that is done
- reporting to the project board or senior managers
- progress and monitoring
- outcomes
- implementation
- monitoring and review

Functional processes that you are involved with or responsible for:

- the recruitment and selection process
- budgeting
- planning
- review of products and services
- training and development
- performance review
- negotiations
- employee resourcing
- managing information systems
- disciplinary and grievance procedures
- health and safety

Certain procedures, for example the compilation of a report:

- the need for the report and its purpose
- your remit
- the people involved
- research methodology
- carrying out research
- analysis of findings
- application of findings
- results
- conclusions
- outcomes

Clearly, compiling a report does not result simply in a completed document. The amount of preparation and work undertaken before it is completed is valuable evidence for proving competence. The event route advocates explaining and evidencing the stages of compilation, decisions you have made, the significance of specific aspects of the work, and so on. As long as the evidence is available, the compilation of a report could meet the requirements of several elements across units within the NVQ.

Taking the event route

There are two approaches to the event route. The first is to familiarise yourself with the NVQ standards and the requirements of each unit, and then match them against events in which you have been involved. The second is to identify events, projects and processes in which you have previously been involved, are currently working on or plan to work on in the future, and then to see how they fit into the standards.

The second method is advocated as it makes the NVQ work for you, particularly if you decide to use current or future areas of work. The NVQ standards can be used to guide your decisions or actions and to inform on what is expected of you.

Getting advice

Your NVQ advisor or mentor will be able to help you match events against the standards. They may advocate the use of some form of grid or matrix to map the stages of a project or process against a particular element's or unit's requirements and use this as a point of reference when undertaking the work and compiling evidence.

For example, if a candidate is responsible for a project, the different stages of that project would form an event route. The candidate could prove her or his competence in a number of different areas because of the diverse nature of the project. In this case, the candidate would put forward various pieces of evidence associated with the project, for example the initial feasibility study, any contracts or objectives, progress reports and the final evaluation.

Supplementary evidence

When it is not possible to obtain performance evidence, you may support your portfolio with supplementary evidence. This can be generated through questioning by an assessor, testimony reports from managers/colleagues/customers, or simulated training activities. Some examples of evidence, described more fully in the next section, are:

■ Written, audio or video records of candidate's answers to assessor's questions.

■ Written testimonies from managers/colleagues/customers.

■ The output from simulated tasks/activities.

■ Personal statements.

The key thing to remember is that supplementary evidence is just that. It should *support*, not *replace*, your performance evidence.

Special 'NVQ' evidence

Most of the evidence we have referred to so far will already be familiar to you, as items such as reports, letters, minutes of meeting etc. are already part of your job. However, a few types of evidence will be unique to your NVQ. In other words, this type of evidence (listed below) will be generated specifically in order to meet the requirements of the qualification.

■ *Observational analysis sheets* – these are a written record of any assessments which take place through observation.

■ *Candidate questioning* – this is a method of generating evidence by questioning the candidate, either face-to-face or in writing.

■ *Witness testimonies* – these are statements made by others as to your performance in the workplace.

■ *Simulations* – any training or development opportunity undertaken outside the candidate's normal job which is undertaken purely to meet the requirements of the NVQ. These can include role-playing activities, assignments etc.

■ *Personal statements* – these are accounts by candidates which detail work activities and performance. They are often needed in order to put performance evidence in context, i.e. to provide the assessor with some background or other necessary additional information/explanation.

Evidence requirements

All the evidence you submit must comply with four main specifications. Your assessor will check that your evidence is:

■ valid

■ authentic

■ current

■ sufficient

Validity

Your assessor must be confident that the evidence you put forward relates to the specific standard it is supposed to support. In other words, is it valid? Does it really prove your competence in that specific area? To take an example, one candidate submitted a copy of the *blank* pro-forma sheet she would use for note making in order to prove that she kept records of client contact meetings. Without any notes written on it, this blank pro-forma did not prove that she actually kept records of her meetings with clients, only that this one piece of paper existed! The situation was easily resolved when the assessor undertook an observational assessment of the actual client contact records, kept in the candidate's office.

Authenticity

The assessor is not only concerned about the validity of your evidence, she or he will also be looking for proof that the evidence is yours and can be linked to you. For example, you may put forward as evidence a report that has been authored by your department. In this case, you should highlight your involvement in the production of the report and back this up with a testimony from a relevant 'witness', for example another member of the team who was also involved in producing it.

Currency

As a general rule, evidence you submit in support of the NVQ standards should be no more than two years old. In certain instances, where the standard relates to something that would be classed as non-routine in your particular job, this rule has to be relaxed. Nevertheless, the important point to remember is that you want to prove that you are competent *now*, not that you were at some point in the distant past!

Sufficiency

The final point about evidence is related to its scope. Some of the performance criteria are longitudinal in nature, which means that you have to prove competence over the period of time specified by the standards. Your evidence would obviously have to reflect this and would have to be sufficient to prove your competence over the specified time period.

Portfolio contents

Your portfolio will consist of a number of items:

- the standards;
- your reflection and analysis;
- your evidence;
- feedback from your assessor.

These components should appear in the form of:

The standards themselves

When submitting your portfolio for assessment you should be sure to include a copy of the standards to which you are to be assessed.

Reflection and analysis sheets

You will have to write a justification supporting why your evidence meets the standards required by the NVQ. This is done on a reflection and analysis sheet, on a PC by PC basis. For an example of a completed reflection and analysis sheet, see Appendix 1.

Evidence referencing system

Your reflection and analysis will refer to a number of different types of evidence, some of which you will want to include in your portfolio (not all evidence may be included in your portfolio since some of it may be assessed by observational assessment). Given the amount of evidence needed to meet the requirements of the NVQ, an evidence referencing system is obviously essential. How you design it is up to you, but bear in mind that a simple system is most effective. As assessors, we know how frustrating it is to be presented with a portfolio whose referencing system is illogical and inaccurate. A straightforward numbering system (1, 2, 3 etc.) works well and any evidence that needs to be added later can be labelled 1a, 1b, 1c, and so on. Dividers can be used to separate evidence at suitable intervals (items 1–10, 11–20, 21–30, etc.).

Cross-referencing

Cross-referencing refers to the ability of one piece of evidence to meet the requirements of more than one performance criterion. You should make use of cross-referencing at every available opportunity. It is surprising how, with a little thought, the amount of evidence you submit can be reduced in this way. When you have identified a piece of evidence for a particular PC/element/unit, flick through forthcoming PCs, elements and units to make sure there isn't something more relevant that would serve both purposes. Some assessors have been complaining of increased petrol costs and back pain incurred by the sheer size of the NVQ portfolios they have to transport and assess! Obviously, reducing the amount of evidence submitted makes things simpler both for you and for your assessor.

Feedback sheets

Your assessor will complete assessment forms that detail her/his decision (competent, not yet competent, insufficient evidence) on each element and unit you put forward for assessment. This feedback may well be augmented by a personal visit by your assessor. Different people have different ways of working, but you must always get feedback in writing as to why you were deemed competent (or not yet competent). We have included an example of a completed assessor's feedback sheet in Appendix 2.

Part Two   Unit Interpretations and How to Use Them

The second part of this book focuses on your achievement of the Management NVQ at Level 4. Each chapter deals with one unit of the qualification, and is split up into the associated elements and performance criteria as laid down by the MCI management standards.

Your ideas
for evidence

Element

Performance
Criterion

Explanation

Interpretation

Candidate
illustration

Event route

Ideas for evidence

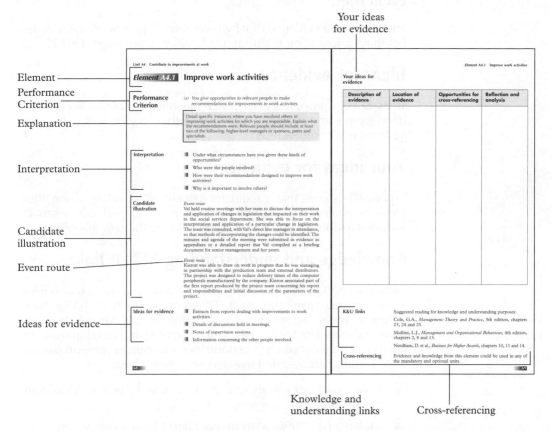

Knowledge and
understanding links

Cross-referencing

An explanation of each performance criterion appears in a tinted panel. The purpose of this explanation is to help you focus on relevant evidence that will enable you to meet the requirements of the standard and to raise the points that need to be covered in your reflection and analysis.

Interpretation

To help you interpret the standard in ways applicable and relevant to your job, we have listed a number of questions you may like to ask yourself. Answering these questions through the use of evidence and analysis will ensure you meet the requirements of the performance criterion.

Candidate illustration

Through our involvement with NVQ candidates we have been able to illustrate how other people have met the requirements of the qualification.

For continuity we have drawn from the experiences and portfolios of four candidates: Kieron, Rosie, Callum and Val. We have chosen them to represent the different organisations in which candidates work. Kieron is a manager in a small software business, Rosie is the manager of a charitable organisation, Callum is a management trainee in a large manufacturing company and, finally, Val is a team manager in the public sector.

Event route

Sometimes the evidence to which we refer is part of an event route. For more information on this type of evidence see pages 19–21.

Ideas for evidence

To assist your processes of evidence identification and collection, we have given some examples of evidence that may be useful, for each performance criterion listed.

Your ideas for evidence

Experience shows that candidates benefit from jotting down their ideas for evidence as they think of them. To support this, we have included a table for you to use while working through this book.

Knowledge and understanding (K&U) links

Getting an NVQ is not just about proving *what* you do. You also need to demonstrate *why* you do it. Different providers of NVQs have different ways of testing your underpinning knowledge and understanding. However, to assist your reading and development, we have cross-referenced each performance criterion to relevant parts of three leading business and management texts. These are:

- Cole, G.A., 1996, *Management: Theory and Practice*, 5th edition, Letts Educational, London.

- Mullins, L.J., 1996, *Management and Organisational Behaviour*, 4th edition, Pitman Publishing, London.

- Needham, D., Dransfield, R., Harris, R., and Coles, M., 1995, *Business for Higher Awards*, Heinemann, Oxford.

We recommend that you have regular access to at least one of these texts.

Cross-referencing

As every portfolio is unique, so too are the opportunities for cross-referencing. Nevertheless, evidence put forward in support of some performance criteria will often be suitable for others. When this is the case, we have listed these opportunities for cross-referencing.

CHAPTER 4

Unit A2 Manage activities to meet requirements

| Element A2.1 | # Implement plans to meet customer requirements |

Performance Criterion

(a) You agree requirements with customers in sufficient detail to allow work to be planned effectively.

To meet the requirements of this PC you will need to detail your knowledge of internal and external customer/client/service user requirements. Explain how these are identified and agreed with customers. Illustrate how these requirements are used to inform the work-planning process.

Interpretation

▉ Who are your customers?

▉ How are their requirements agreed?

▉ How are these requirements used to plan work?

Candidate illustration

Event route
Kieron focused on contracting orders with customers for this element. Customer requirements for particular components and grades of computer programs were identified and agreed using standardised order forms and contracts. These documents allowed Kieron to schedule delivery and installation plans to suit customer requirements. Kieron fully explained this in his analysis and highlighted examples of contracts and orders made with customers as evidence.

Event route
Val detailed the care-planning process throughout this element. Care plans completed in discussion with clients were included as evidence. In her analysis, Val explained the care-planning process and how she oversees it. Actual care plans for individual clients were submitted as evidence. To maintain organisational confidentiality requirements, the names of the clients and the dates of the plans were deleted.

Ideas for evidence

▉ Details of customer requirements.

▉ Completed pro-formas.

▉ Contracted agreements.

▉ Plans for service delivery.

Your ideas for evidence

Description of evidence	Location of evidence	Opportunities for cross-referencing	Reflection and analysis

K&U links	Suggested reading for knowledge and understanding purposes:
	Cole, G.A., *Management: Theory and Practice,* 5th edition, chapters 19, 21 and 26.
	Mullins, L.J., *Management and Organisational Behaviour,* 4th edition, chapters 9 and 13, pp. 453–5.
	Needham, D. et al., *Business for Higher Awards*, chapter 10.
Cross-referencing	Evidence and knowledge from this element can be used in the following mandatory units of NVQ Management Level 4: **A4, C2, C5, B2, D4**; and the following optional units: **C10, C13, C15, D2, F2, F4, F6, F7, G1**.

Element A2.1 Implement plans to meet customer requirements

Performance Criterion

(b) *Your plans allow requirements to be met within agreed timescales.*

> You should link to previous PC, if appropriate. Your plans should encompass all of the following kinds of requirements throughout this element: quality, quantity, delivery, and health and safety. Focus on specific work plans and explain the appropriateness of timescales.

Interpretation

◼ How are work plans recorded?

◼ What detail is provided?

◼ How are timescales established?

Candidate illustration

Event route
Kieron continued to focus on contracted agreements with customers. Timescales are of the highest importance, both to customers and Kieron's organisation, because of production, warehousing and distribution considerations and other legislation. Kieron explained his remit as the sales manager in coordinating this area with customers. As evidence he included the requested timescales from customers and evidence of communications with internal departments to ensure that they were met.

Event route
Val continued to focus on the care-planning process, involving clients with service providers to ensure the provision of appropriate care based on client need and assessment. Timescales for periods of care are an integral part of this process and Val was able to cross-reference to evidence used for PC (a) of this element.

Ideas for evidence

◼ Cross-reference to existing evidence, if appropriate.

◼ Details of timescales agreed with customers:
  – programmes;
  – contracts;
  – service delivery plans.

◼ Details of organisational plans designed to meet timescales:
  – production;
  – preparation;
  – storage;
  – delivery.

Your ideas for evidence

Description of evidence	Location of evidence	Opportunities for cross-referencing	Reflection and analysis

K&U links

Suggested reading for knowledge and understanding purposes:

Cole, G.A., *Management: Theory and Practice*, 5th edition, chapters 19, 21 and 26.

Mullins, L.J., *Management and Organisational Behaviour*, 4th edition, chapters 9 and 13, pp. 453–5.

Needham, D. et al., *Business for Higher Awards*, chapter 10.

Cross-referencing

Evidence and knowledge from this element can be used in the following mandatory units of NVQ Management Level 4: **A4, C2, C5, B2, D4**; and the following optional units: **C10, C13, C15, D2, F2, F4, F6, F7, G1**.

Element A2.1 Implement plans to meet customer requirements

Performance Criterion

(c) You explain plans to relevant people in sufficient detail and at an appropriate level and pace.

> Again, focus on specific work plans that have been designed to meet customers' requirements. Illustrate how you have used your communication skills and knowledge to provide the relevant people with the information in the most appropriate way. Relevant people should include at least one of the following: team members, peers, higher-level managers or sponsors, and people outside your organisation.

Interpretation

◼ How are work plans explained to those involved?

◼ Does your prior knowledge of these people impact on your method of communication?

◼ How much detail is required?

Candidate illustration

Event route
Kieron cross-referenced to the evidence used for PC (b) of this element. In his analysis he highlighted examples of specific memos and information he had sent to departmental managers to explain how he had tailored the information to suit their needs. Pro-formas were also included, and Kieron explained why standardised systems of communication had been developed.

Event route
Callum cross-referenced to evidence originally referenced in Unit C2, Element C2.2, PC (g), where he was required to plan for an extra order of drilling products from a major distributor. The evidence detailed meetings Callum held with production managers to plan the production of customer requirements.

Ideas for evidence

◼ Cross-reference to existing evidence, if appropriate.

◼ Details of communication with others involved in the production or service delivery process.

◼ Examples of the plans that you had to explain.

◼ Witness testimony from others involved confirming your actions.

Your ideas for evidence

Description of evidence	Location of evidence	Opportunities for cross-referencing	Reflection and analysis

K&U links

Suggested reading for knowledge and understanding purposes:

Cole, G.A., *Management: Theory and Practice,* 5th edition, chapters 19, 21 and 26.

Mullins, L.J., *Management and Organisational Behaviour,* 4th edition, chapters 9 and 13, pp. 453–5.

Needham, D. et al., *Business for Higher Awards,* chapter 10.

Cross-referencing

Evidence and knowledge from this element can be used in the following mandatory units of NVQ Management Level 4: **A4, C2, C5, B2, D4**; and the following optional units: **C10, C13, C15, D2, F2, F4, F6, F7, G1**.

Element A2.1   Implement plans to meet customer requirements

Performance Criterion

(d) You confirm with relevant people their understanding of, and commitment to, your plans.

> Link to the previous performance criterion, if appropriate. Continuing with your plans to meet customer requirements, illustrate how you have clarified people's understanding when communicating plans. Explain how you have obtained their commitment to plans.

Interpretation

■ Who are relevant people?

■ When communicating plans to meet customer requirements, how do you ensure that they are understood?

■ How do you obtain commitment from others to your plans?

Candidate illustration

Event route
Both Kieron and Callum were able to cross-reference to the evidence used in PC (c) of this element. In their analysis they detailed the replies received from their original communications, showing acceptance and understanding of the plans. Additional minutes of relevant meetings held were also submitted.

Ideas for evidence

■ Cross-reference to existing evidence if required.

■ Details of replies to your correspondence.

■ Minutes of meetings where plans have been discussed and agreed.

■ Witness testimony from others involved.

Your ideas for evidence

Description of evidence	Location of evidence	Opportunities for cross-referencing	Reflection and analysis

K&U links

Suggested reading for knowledge and understanding purposes:

Cole, G.A., *Management: Theory and Practice,* 5th edition, chapters 19, 21 and 26.

Mullins, L.J., *Management and Organisational Behaviour,* 4th edition, chapters 9 and 13, pp. 453–5.

Needham, D. et al., *Business for Higher Awards,* chapter 10.

Cross-referencing

Evidence and knowledge from this element can be used in the following mandatory units of NVQ Management Level 4: **A4, C2, C5, B2, D4**; and the following optional units: **C10, C13, C15, D2, F2, F4, F6, F7, G1**.

Element A2.1 | Implement plans to meet customer requirements

Performance Criterion

(e) You follow organisational procedures for recording your plans.

Detail the relevant organisational procedures that impact on your recording of plans of work which are designed to meet customer requirements. These procedures may have been designed to comply with internal policy, legislation or in-house systems.

Interpretation

▰ What organisational procedures dictate methods of recording plans?

▰ How are plans recorded?

Candidate illustration

Event route
Val continued to focus on the care-planning process. The department's procedures for care planning incorporated standardised documentation. Completed examples of care plans were cross-referenced from PC (a). In her analysis she detailed the organisational procedures that underpin the care-planning documentation.

Event route
Kieron detailed the standardised contracts used by the organisation when accepting orders. The contracts were cross-referenced from PC (a) and Kieron detailed the organisational procedures in his analysis.

Ideas for evidence

▰ Examples of compliance with procedures.

▰ Completed pro-formas.

▰ Completed contracts.

▰ Excerpts and examples of relevant organisational procedures.

Your ideas for evidence

Description of evidence	Location of evidence	Opportunities for cross-referencing	Reflection and analysis

K&U links

Suggested reading for knowledge and understanding purposes:

Cole, G.A., *Management: Theory and Practice*, 5th edition, chapters 19, 21 and 26.

Mullins, L.J., *Management and Organisational Behaviour*, 4th edition, chapters 9 and 13, pp. 453–5.

Needham, D. et al., *Business for Higher Awards*, chapter 10.

Cross-referencing

Evidence and knowledge from this element can be used in the following mandatory units of NVQ Management Level 4: **A4, C2, C5, B2, D4**; and the following optional units: **C10, C13, C15, D2, F2, F4, F6, F7, G1**.

Element A2.1 Implement plans to meet customer requirements

Performance Criterion

(f) You give opportunities to relevant people to make recommendations for improving plans.

> Focus on specific instances where you have provided these kinds of opportunities. Explain who the relevant people were and the kinds of opportunities provided. Illustrate how their input improved plans under discussion.

Interpretation

■ Who were the relevant people involved?

■ How did you provide opportunities for those people to suggest improvements to plans?

■ How have their suggestions improved plans to meet customer requirements?

Candidate illustration

Event route
Callum cross-referenced to the evidence used for PC (c) of this element. Contained in the minutes of meetings with the production manager were instances where he had encouraged technical staff to make suggestions for improvement to the components and machinery used in the manufacturing of the special order. Callum highlighted these and explained their significance in improving plans.

Event route
Kieron routinely consulted all managers, peers and customers when ensuring that customer requirements would be met. He was able to evidence this using minutes of meetings with staff and correspondence exchanged with customers.

Ideas for evidence

■ Cross-reference to existing evidence where appropriate.

■ Minutes of meetings with relevant people, during which recommendations were made.

■ Correspondence with appropriate people.

■ Witness testimony from appropriate people confirming that opportunities were given.

■ Outcomes from company suggestion schemes, etc.

Your ideas for evidence

Description of evidence	Location of evidence	Opportunities for cross-referencing	Reflection and analysis

K&U links

Suggested reading for knowledge and understanding purposes:

Cole, G.A., *Management: Theory and Practice*, 5th edition, chapters 19, 21 and 26.

Mullins, L.J., *Management and Organisational Behaviour*, 4th edition, chapters 9 and 13, pp. 453–5.

Needham, D. et al., *Business for Higher Awards*, chapter 10.

Cross-referencing

Evidence and knowledge from this element can be used in the following mandatory units of NVQ Management Level 4: **A4**, **C2**, **C5**, **B2**, **D4**; and the following optional units: **C10**, **C13**, **C15**, **D2**, **F2**, **F4**, **F6**, **F7**, **G1**.

| *Element A2.2* | # Maintain a healthy, safe and productive work environment |

Performance Criterion

(a) *You inform relevant people about their legal and organisational responsibilities for maintaining a healthy, safe and productive work environment.*

> To meet the requirements of this PC you will need to explain your role in ensuring a healthy, safe and productive environment at work. Detail specific instances where you have provided information about this to relevant people. Relevant people should include at least two of the following: team members, peers, higher-level managers, sponsors, and people from outside your organisation. Your evidence throughout this element should cover the following features of the work environment: physical environment, equipment, materials and working procedures.

Interpretation

▌ Why is it important to inform people of their responsibility for health and safety issues?

▌ How do you do this?

▌ Why can these kinds of issues impact on productivity levels?

Candidate illustration

Event route

As a member of the Investors in People (IIP) steering group, Val had responsibility for undertaking a health and safety audit of the district office in which she worked. Part of her responsibility was to inform all the teams using the office of the reasons for the audit, the audit criteria and the nature of the work being carried out. As evidence, Val included in her portfolio the memo sent to all office users and a series of posters that she had designed and pinned to notice boards around the building.

Event route

On studying this element, Rosie found that the working environment for which she was responsible did not comply with relevant legislation. She called a staff meeting in response to discuss organisational requirements as published in the in-house procedures file. As a result of this meeting, a number of gaps between legal and organisational requirements were found. Rosie included the minutes of this meeting and its agenda as evidence. Owing to the sensitive nature of this evidence, Rosie invited her assessor to view the minutes of this meeting on site rather than include it in her portfolio of evidence.

Ideas for evidence

▌ Relevant communications.

▌ Materials you have displayed (leaflets, posters etc.).

▌ Agendas and minutes of relevant meetings.

Your ideas for evidence

Description of evidence	Location of evidence	Opportunities for cross-referencing	Reflection and analysis

K&U links

Suggested reading for knowledge and understanding purposes:

Cole, G.A., *Management: Theory and Practice*, 5th edition, chapter 50, pp. 403–4.

Any health and safety/risk assessment text.

Cross-referencing

Evidence and knowledge from this element can be used in the following mandatory units of NVQ Management Level 4: **A4, C2, C5, B2, D4**; and the following optional units: **C10, C13, C15, D2, F2, F4, F6, F7, G1**.

Element A2.2 Maintain a healthy, safe and productive work environment

Performance Criterion

(b) You make sufficient support available to relevant people to ensure they can work in a healthy, safe and productive way.

> To meet the requirements of this PC you will need to explain how you have supported others to ensure that a safe working environment is maintained. Detail any resources, advice or information that you have provided.

Interpretation

▌ What are your responsibilities regarding health and safety?

▌ What kind of support have you provided to others?

▌ How did this support help to ensure that people work in a healthy, safe and productive way?

Candidate illustration

Event route
Val focused on the outcomes of the safety audit she undertook and evidenced some of the new equipment provided as a result (anti-glare screens for computers and adjustable chairs for computer operators).

Event route
Rosie continued to focus on the work that needed to be done to improve the office environment to bring it in line with the requirements of legislation. To improve health and safety in the workplace, Rosie introduced an employees' ideas scheme. She included the promotional literature that she had developed and explained, in a personal statement, that each idea was actioned where practical. Examples of some of the ideas that had been implemented were also included.

Ideas for evidence

▌ Documents detailing support provided:
  – requests for information and equipment;
  – responses to requests (delivery notes, memos, emails etc.).

▌ Examples of support provided:
  – witness testimony;
  – photographic evidence.

Your ideas for evidence

Description of evidence	Location of evidence	Opportunities for cross-referencing	Reflection and analysis

K&U links Suggested reading for knowledge and understanding purposes:

Cole, G.A., *Management: Theory and Practice*, 5th edition, chapter 50, pp. 403–4.

Any health and safety/risk assessment text.

Cross-referencing Evidence and knowledge from this element can be used in the following mandatory units of NVQ Management Level 4: **A4, C2, C5, B2, D4**; and the following optional units: **C10, C13, C15, D2, F2, F4, F6, F7, G1**.

Element A2.2 Maintain a healthy, safe and productive work environment

Performance Criterion

(c) You provide opportunities for relevant people to make recommendations for improving the work environment.

To meet the requirements of this PC you will need to detail instances where you have provided these opportunities. If you can, highlight examples where these opportunities have led to actual improvements in the working environment.

Interpretation

- How have you provided opportunities?
- Who were the relevant people?
- What kinds of suggestions were forthcoming?
- What was (were) the outcome(s)?

Candidate illustration

Event route
Val was able to utilise the agenda and minutes of meetings used in PC (a). She highlighted the ideas put forward in the minutes and explained their significance in her analysis.

Event route
Rosie was able to reference PC (b), her introduction of the employees' ideas scheme.

Ideas for evidence

- Cross-reference to previous evidence used in this element, if appropriate.
- Agendas and minutes of meetings where ideas have been requested and submitted.
- Details of any ideas schemes in operation and examples of ideas put forward.
- Supervision records.

Your ideas for evidence

Description of evidence	Location of evidence	Opportunities for cross-referencing	Reflection and analysis

K&U links

Suggested reading for knowledge and understanding purposes:

Cole, G.A., *Management: Theory and Practice*, 5th edition, chapter 50, pp. 403–4.

Any health and safety/risk assessment text.

Cross-referencing

Evidence and knowledge from this element can be used in the following mandatory units of NVQ Management Level 4: **A4**, **C2**, **C5**, **B2**, **D4**; and the following optional units: **C10**, **C13**, **C15**, **D2**, **F2**, **F4**, **F6**, **F7**, **G1**.

Element A2.2 Maintain a healthy, safe and productive work environment

Performance Criterion

(d) The work environment under your control conforms to organisational and legal requirements.

> To meet the requirements of this PC you will need to explain any legal and organisational requirements that impact upon your work environment. Detail any actions you have taken to ensure that your working environment complies with these.

Interpretation

▪ Which legal and organisational requirements concerning health and safety impact upon your particular working environment?

▪ How do you ensure compliance with these requirements?

Candidate illustration

Event route
Val submitted the audit documentation referred to in PC (a). It highlighted compliance and non-compliance with requirements. She also included an action plan designed to ensure that the necessary improvements were made and a witness testimony from her line manager confirming that the action points had been implemented, ensuring requirements were now met.

Event route
Rosie also detailed the improvements that had been made as a result of the meeting detailed in PC (a). She explained in a personal report that an external supplier of computerised and electronic equipment had been contracted to undertake a regular inspection of equipment. She also invited her assessor to the workplace to see that it now complied with all health and safety requirements. Her assessor documented this in an observational assessment report.

Ideas for evidence

▪ Cross-reference to previous evidence used in this element, if appropriate.

▪ Details of changes and improvements made in line with legal and organisational requirements.

▪ Observational assessment report from your assessor.

▪ Personal report detailing action taken.

Your ideas for evidence

Description of evidence	Location of evidence	Opportunities for cross-referencing	Reflection and analysis

K&U links

Suggested reading for knowledge and understanding purposes:

Cole, G.A., *Management: Theory and Practice*, 5th edition, chapter 50, pp. 403–4.

Any health and safety/risk assessment text.

Cross-referencing

Evidence and knowledge from this element can be used in the following mandatory units of NVQ Management Level 4: **A4**, **C2**, **C5**, **B2**, **D4**; and the following optional units: **C10**, **C13**, **C15**, **D2**, **F2**, **F4**, **F6**, **F7**, **G1**.

Element A2.2	# Maintain a healthy, safe and productive work environment

Performance Criterion

(e) *The work environment under your control is as conducive to healthy, safe and productive working as possible within organisational constraints.*

> We suggest that you link to the previous PC, if appropriate. You should provide specific examples where you have taken action to ensure that your working environment is conducive to safe working. Detail any organisational constraints that have impacted upon your actions.

Interpretation

▉ What actions have you taken in order to create or maintain a safe and healthy working environment?

▉ How have organisational constraints (time, money, your level of authority etc.) limited or dictated your actions?

Candidate illustration

Event route
Val cross-referenced to the interventions made in PCs (a), (b), (c) and (d). In her analysis, Val highlighted the fact that health and safety was an ongoing issue and that she had promoted the concept of shared responsibilities throughout. On its own, this evidence was deemed insufficient to meet the requirements of this PC. Her assessor asked Val to explain and evidence how organisational requirements had impacted upon her actions. Val re-submitted this element, along with additional budgetary information and suppliers' estimates for equipment. All the equipment purchased had to be funded from her existing office budget. She demonstrated that as one supplier's estimate was outside budgetary constraints, she chose the supplier whose estimate was affordable (i.e. within the financial constraints).

Event route
Rosie cross-referenced to evidence of her assessor's observation used in PC (d). Her analysis emphasised the financial constraints on her organisation and examined the difficulties experienced in ensuring a safe working environment because of these constraints.

Ideas for evidence

▉ Cross-reference to existing evidence used in this element, if appropriate.

▉ Details of internal and external audits undertaken.

▉ Observational assessment outcomes.

▉ Evidence of relevant organisational constraints.

▉ Personal report detailing your actions.

▉ Witness testimonies from others involved.

Your ideas for evidence

Description of evidence	Location of evidence	Opportunities for cross-referencing	Reflection and analysis

K&U links

Suggested reading for knowledge and understanding purposes:

Cole, G.A., *Management: Theory and Practice*, 5th edition, chapter 50, pp. 403–4.

Any health and safety/risk assessment text.

Cross-referencing

Evidence and knowledge from this element can be used in the following mandatory units of NVQ Management Level 4: **A4, C2, C5, B2, D4**; and the following optional units: **C10, C13, C15, D2, F2, F4, F6, F7, G1**.

Element A2.2

Maintain a healthy, safe and productive work environment

Performance Criterion

(f) You respond to breaches in health and safety requirements promptly and in line with organisational and legal requirements.

> We suggest that you link to the previous PC, if appropriate. Explain specific instances where requirements have been breached and the actions you have taken to resolve them. Identify any organisational and legal requirements that have informed your actions.

Interpretation

▌ What kinds of breaches have occurred?

▌ How have you responded; what action have you taken?

▌ What (if any) timescales were significant?

▌ Which organisational and legal requirements were relevant?

Candidate illustration

Event route
Both Val and Rosie cross-referenced to evidence used throughout this element. They highlighted how breaches were identified (through audit), ideas for improvements, relevant organisational and legal requirements, and the actions taken.

Ideas for evidence

▌ Cross-reference to existing evidence used in this element, if appropriate.

▌ Details of how breaches are identified (for example, routine checks).

▌ Actions that you have taken in response.

▌ Memos.

▌ Reports.

▌ Records of improvements made.

▌ Receipts from suppliers who have made these improvements.

▌ Personal report detailing your actions.

▌ Witness testimonies from others involved.

Your ideas for evidence

Description of evidence	Location of evidence	Opportunities for cross-referencing	Reflection and analysis

K&U links

Suggested reading for knowledge and understanding purposes:

Cole, G.A., *Management: Theory and Practice*, 5th edition, chapter 50, pp. 403–4.

Any health and safety/risk assessment text.

Cross-referencing

Evidence and knowledge from this element can be used in the following mandatory units of NVQ Management Level 4: **A4, C2, C5, B2, D4**; and the following optional units: **C10, C13, C15, D2, F2, F4, F6, F7, G1**.

Element A2.2   Maintain a healthy, safe and productive work environment

Performance Criterion

(g) You make recommendations for improving the work environment clearly and promptly to relevant people.

> You will need to detail instances where you have made recommendations for improving the physical working environment, equipment and materials or working procedures. Explain how these recommendations were made and identify the people to whom they were made.

Interpretation

■ What kinds of recommendations have you made?

■ Why were they made?

■ How were the recommendations made?

■ Who were the recipients of your recommendations?

Candidate illustration

Event route
Val cross-referenced to her audit documentation, evidenced in PCs (a) and (b). She showed that the outcomes, recommendations and action plan that formed part of the audit were forwarded to her line manager and to the finance section for approval prior to changes being made. Val also obtained a testimony from her finance manager confirming that she had complied with organisational requirements by submitting the proposal.

Event route
Rosie cross-referenced to evidence she had put forward so far. Through her comparison of organisational and legal requirements, it was clear that her organisation did not meet all its responsibilities under relevant legislation. As a result, Rosie sent her district manager copies of the audits, in-house procedures and legal requirements as well as a report detailing the improvements she needed to make. She suggested that all this information be shared with other area offices to ensure that the entire organisation met health and safety requirements.

Ideas for evidence

■ Cross-reference to existing evidence used in this element, if appropriate.

■ Details of recommendations made:
 – memos;
 – reports;
 – any other correspondence.

■ Details of people to whom recommendations are made and why they are appropriate.

Your ideas for evidence

Description of evidence	Location of evidence	Opportunities for cross-referencing	Reflection and analysis

K&U links

Suggested reading for knowledge and understanding purposes:

Cole, G.A., *Management: Theory and Practice*, 5th edition, chapter 50, pp. 403–4.

Any health and safety/risk assessment text.

Cross-referencing

Evidence and knowledge from this element can be used in the following mandatory units of NVQ Management Level 4: **A4, C2, C5, B2, D4**; and the following optional units: **C10, C13, C15, D2, F2, F4, F6, F7, G1**.

Element A2.2 Maintain a healthy, safe and productive work environment

Performance Criterion

(h) Your records regarding health and safety and the work environment are complete, accurate and comply with organisational and legal requirements.

> You will need to provide examples of your records and record-keeping systems, and explain their utility. Don't forget to detail the organisational and legal requirements to which the records relate.

Interpretation

▎ What kinds of health and safety records are kept?

▎ How do you ensure that they are complete and accurate?

▎ How are these records used to demonstrate compliance with organisational and legal requirements?

Candidate illustration

Event route
Val kept records of the improvements she had made as a result of her audit (PCs (a)–(g)), and included these and the audit as evidence. Although her assessor agreed that the audit was an example of a complete and accurate record, for health and safety purposes she felt that more evidence was needed. Val submitted some extracts from the accident book, which demonstrated that she had kept accurate and complete records, in line with legal requirements.

Event route
Rosie included photocopied extracts from the office visitors' book, showing that the occupancy of the building was monitored in line with health and safety and fire regulations. Like Val, she also submitted extracts from the office accident book, explaining how it was designed to comply with organisational and legal requirements.

Ideas for evidence

▎ Cross-reference to existing evidence used in this element, if appropriate.

▎ Examples of records kept.

▎ Explanations of record design and storage.

▎ Details of organisational and legal requirements that impact upon recording techniques.

Your ideas for evidence

Description of evidence	Location of evidence	Opportunities for cross-referencing	Reflection and analysis

K&U links

Suggested reading for knowledge and understanding purposes:

Cole, G.A., *Management: Theory and Practice,* 5th edition, chapter 50, pp. 403–4.

Any health and safety/risk assessment text.

Cross-referencing

Evidence and knowledge from this element can be used in the following mandatory units of NVQ Management Level 4: **A4, C2, C5, B2, D4**; and the following optional units: **C10, C13, C15, D2, F2, F4, F6, F7, G1**.

Element A2.3 Ensure products and services meet quality requirements

Performance Criterion

(a) *You give opportunities to relevant people to monitor the quality of products and services and recommend improvements to the processes involved.*

> Explain how opportunities of this nature are provided. Illustrate competence by detailing the kinds of recommendations that are made. Relevant people should include at least two of the following throughout this element: team members, peers, higher-level managers, or sponsors and specialists. Requirements should include all of the following throughout this element: quality standards, organisational policies and organisational objectives.

Interpretation

- How do you give these kinds of opportunities?
- Do they occur routinely?
- What kinds of recommendations have been made?

Candidate illustration

Event route
Kieron focused on the after-sales services provided by his department. He submitted completed examples of post-sales questionnaires sent to customers and detailed the actions taken in response to the information and data they provided. Kieron also detailed in a personal report the relevant people involved in making improvements.

Event route
As part of her job role, Val was chair of a local service user and provider forum that reviewed social services and multi-agency service provision. She detailed the other members of the forum, including service users, representatives from social services, the local health authority and district councillors. She also included minutes of meetings with the forum detailing proposed changes to services made by other members.

Ideas for evidence

- Minutes of meetings where service and product quality has been discussed.
- Personal report detailing the status of the others involved.
- Examples of completed in-house and external questionnaires designed to give feedback regarding quality.
- Witness testimony from relevant people.

Your ideas for evidence

Description of evidence	Location of evidence	Opportunities for cross-referencing	Reflection and analysis

K&U links

Suggested reading for knowledge and understanding purposes:

Cole, G.A., *Management: Theory and Practice,* 5th edition, chapters 6, 8 and 29.

Needham, D. et al., *Business for Higher Awards*, chapter 10.

Cross-referencing

Evidence and knowledge from this element can be used in the following mandatory units of NVQ Management Level 4: **A4**, **C5**, **D4**, **B2**; and the following optional units: **D2**, **F2**, **F4**, **F6**, **F7**.

| Element A2.3 | # Ensure products and services meet quality requirements |

Performance Criterion

(b) *Your monitoring of the quality of products and services is continuous and complies with your organisation's procedures.*

> Link to PC (c), if appropriate. Detail your responsibility for the monitoring of the products or services that you provide. Explain the process and detail any organisational procedures that impact on your actions.

Interpretation

▪ How do you continuously monitor the quality of products and services?

▪ Which organisational procedures are relevant?

Candidate illustration

Event route
Kieron cross-referenced to the evidence used in PC (a) of this element. He explained that a questionnaire was forwarded to customers following any provision of products and services to ensure that constant feedback was obtained. He also evidenced the in-house quality assurance systems used to monitor delivery times, and submitted statistics comparing forecasted and actual delivery times.

Event route
Callum cross-referenced to Unit D4, Element D4.2, PC (e), where he was responsible for improving the quality assurance monitoring systems used on a production line. He evidenced the report subsequently submitted to senior management, outlining the system and emphasising its significance in reducing faulty products and the economic benefits inherent in adopting his proposals for improvement.

Ideas for evidence

▪ Cross-reference to existing evidence, if appropriate.

▪ Details of the systems in place:
 – records of monitoring;
 – dates and times that monitoring occurs;
 – statistics produced.

▪ Reports detailing monitoring systems.

▪ Questionnaires and other methods used to obtain data and information.

Your ideas for evidence

Description of evidence	Location of evidence	Opportunities for cross-referencing	Reflection and analysis

K&U links

Suggested reading for knowledge and understanding purposes:

Cole, G.A., *Management: Theory and Practice*, 5th edition, chapters 6, 8 and 29.

Needham, D. et al., *Business for Higher Awards*, chapter 10.

Cross-referencing

Evidence and knowledge from this element can be used in the following mandatory units of NVQ Management Level 4: **A4**, **C5**, **D4**, **B2**; and the following optional units: **D2**, **F2**, **F4**, **F6**, **F7**.

| Element A2.3 | # Ensure products and services meet quality requirements |

Performance Criterion

(c) *The products and services within your area of responsibility consistently meet your customers' and organisation's requirements.*

> Link to the previous PC, if appropriate. Following on from the monitoring of products and services, explain how you ensure that quality is maintained according to internal and external requirements.

Interpretation

■ How do you consistently maintain the quality of products and services?

■ How do internal and external requirements inform on product and service quality?

Candidate illustration

Event route
Kieron was able to cross-reference to the evidence used in PCs (a) and (b), where customer questionnaires had been distributed and returned. In his analysis, Kieron explained that the questionnaire had been approved by his organisation. He also provided evidence of how the completed questionnaires were used by in-house quality circle teams to review methods of production, the range of components used, logistical considerations, sales techniques and customer service. Minutes from several quality circle team meetings were used in evidence and Kieron annotated them to highlight the relevant areas and discussions that occurred.

Event route
Callum submitted statistics that were collated as a result of the implementation of his quality assurance monitoring system, detailed in PC (b). The statistics showed improvements in production times and a reduction in the number of faulty products returned by customers. He obtained a witness testimony from his line manager, confirming that his work contributed to the achievement of organisational objectives and was supportive of organisational procedures.

Ideas for evidence

■ Cross-reference to existing evidence, if appropriate.

■ Details of monitoring systems.

■ Outcomes of monitoring.

■ An explanation of the organisational requirements that impact on product and service quality.

Your ideas for evidence

Description of evidence	Location of evidence	Opportunities for cross-referencing	Reflection and analysis

K&U links

Suggested reading for knowledge and understanding purposes:

Cole, G.A., *Management: Theory and Practice*, 5th edition, chapters 6, 8 and 29.

Needham, D. et al., *Business for Higher Awards*, chapter 10.

Cross-referencing

Evidence and knowledge from this element can be used in the following mandatory units of NVQ Management Level 4: **A4**, **C5**, **D4**, **B2**; and the following optional units: **D2**, **F2**, **F4**, **F6**, **F7**.

Element A2.3	# Ensure products and services meet quality requirements

Performance Criterion

(d) Where products, services and the processes involved do not meet agreed requirements, you take prompt and effective action.

> Detail specific instances where the products and services within your area of responsibility have failed to meet quality standards. Explain the circumstances and the actions you have taken to rectify the situation.

Interpretation

▌ Under what circumstances have agreed requirements not been met?

▌ What action did you take?

Candidate illustration

Event route
Val detailed issues raised in the service user and provider forum (see PC (a)), where the allocation of services to a particular user was found to be inappropriate and did not meet their requirements. As that particular service relied on the input of an external agency as well as social services, Val convened a meeting with the other agency to review the service user's needs and to reallocate the necessary personnel and resources. Minutes of the forum discussion and subsequent review meeting were submitted as evidence. Val annotated the minutes to highlight the relevant points made.

Event route
Kieron evidenced an incident where a product sent to a customer was incompatible with their computerised information system, despite reassurances from Kieron's company that it was compatible. Kieron provided evidence of the action taken through correspondence with the client, apologising for the error and offering an alternative with free on-site maintenance as a form of service recovery.

Ideas for evidence

▌ Details of the nature of non-compliance with requirements.

▌ Evidence of actions taken:
 – correspondence;
 – minutes of meetings.

▌ Personal report detailing the circumstances and the actions taken.

Your ideas for evidence

Description of evidence	Location of evidence	Opportunities for cross-referencing	Reflection and analysis

K&U links Suggested reading for knowledge and understanding purposes:

Cole, G.A., *Management: Theory and Practice*, 5th edition, chapters 6, 8 and 29.

Needham, D. et al., *Business for Higher Awards*, chapter 10.

Cross-referencing Evidence and knowledge from this element can be used in the following mandatory units of NVQ Management Level 4: **A4**, **C5**, **D4**, **B2**; and the following optional units: **D2**, **F2**, **F4**, **F6**, **F7**.

Ensure products and services meet quality requirements

Performance Criterion

(e) *Your records relating to the quality of products and services comply with your organisation's procedures.*

> Explain specific records that represent the monitoring of quality. Detail their utility and how they comply with your organisation's procedures.

Interpretation

■ What kinds of quality monitoring records are kept?

■ How are those records used?

■ What organisational procedures impact on these kinds of records?

Candidate illustration

Event route
Both Kieron and Callum were able to cross-reference to records evidenced throughout this element, for example customer questionnaires and statistics relating to production. Each was explained and details of organisational procedures were submitted in the form of a personal statement.

Ideas for evidence

■ Cross-reference to existing evidence, if appropriate.

■ Examples of completed records that are used to monitor the quality of products and services.

■ Explanations of your organisation's procedures regarding quality documentation.

Your ideas for evidence

Description of evidence	Location of evidence	Opportunities for cross-referencing	Reflection and analysis

K&U links

Suggested reading for knowledge and understanding purposes:

Cole, G.A., *Management: Theory and Practice*, 5th edition, chapters 6, 8 and 29.

Needham, D. et al., *Business for Higher Awards*, chapter 10.

Cross-referencing

Evidence and knowledge from this element can be used in the following mandatory units of NVQ Management Level 4: **A4**, **C5**, **D4**, **B2**; and the following optional units: **D2**, **F2**, **F4**, **F6**, **F7**.

CHAPTER 5

Unit A4 Contribute to improvements at work

Element A4.1   Improve work activities

Performance Criterion

(a) You give opportunities to relevant people to make recommendations for improvements to work activities.

> Detail specific instances where you have involved others in improving work activities for which you are responsible. Explain what the recommendations were. Relevant people should include at least two of the following: higher-level managers or sponsors, peers and specialists.

Interpretation

▌ Under what circumstances have you given these kinds of opportunities?

▌ Who were the people involved?

▌ How were their recommendations designed to improve work activities?

▌ Why is it important to involve others?

Candidate illustration

Event route

Val held routine meetings with her team to discuss the interpretation and application of changes in legislation that impacted on their work in the social services department. She was able to focus on the interpretation and application of a particular change in legislation. The team was consulted, with Val's direct line manager in attendance, so that methods of incorporating the changes could be identified. The minutes and agenda of the meeting were submitted in evidence as appendixes to a detailed report that Val compiled as a briefing document for senior management and her peers.

Event route

Kieron was able to draw on work in progress that he was managing in partnership with the production team and external distributors. The project was designed to reduce delivery times of the computer peripherals manufactured by the company. Kieron annotated part of the first report produced by the project team concerning his report and responsibilities and initial discussion of the parameters of the project.

Ideas for evidence

▌ Extracts from reports dealing with improvements to work activities.

▌ Details of discussions held in meetings.

▌ Notes of supervision sessions.

▌ Information concerning the other people involved.

Your ideas for evidence

Description of evidence	Location of evidence	Opportunities for cross-referencing	Reflection and analysis

K&U links

Suggested reading for knowledge and understanding purposes:

Cole, G.A., *Management: Theory and Practice*, 5th edition, chapters 23, 24 and 25.

Mullins, L.J., *Management and Organisational Behaviour*, 4th edition, chapters 2, 8 and 15.

Needham, D. et al., *Business for Higher Awards*, chapters 10, 11 and 14.

Cross-referencing

Evidence and knowledge from this element could be used in any of the mandatory and optional units.

Element A4.1   Improve work activities

Performance Criterion

(b) Your monitoring of activities occurs at intervals most likely to identify potential improvements.

> Read PC (c) prior to undertaking this one. Focus on how and when you monitor work activities. Explain why the timescales used are appropriate and justify your methods of monitoring. Methods should include at least two of the following types of monitoring: direct observation; considering oral information; considering written information.

Interpretation

- How do you monitor work activities?
- What are the timescales involved?
- In what ways is monitoring used to improve work activities?

Candidate illustration

Event route
As part of her job as fundraising manager, Rosie regularly monitored funds raised by volunteers from each fundraising event or activity. This information was used to inform on the most popular kinds of events and activities and to identify best practices for fundraising guidelines. Rosie annotated part of a report, written for senior management approval which identified best practice, for evidence here.

Event route
As a newly appointed trainee manager, Callum was regularly moved between departments to gain experience of their operation. Each department gave him a specific project to improve his practices and benefit the department concerned. In his six months in the marketing department, his project involved market research into the effectiveness of promotional and advisory campaigns launched in the UK. The purpose of his report was to identify improvements in marketing campaigns specifically aimed at the extractive industry. Callum was able to annotate extracts from the final project report to meet all the requirements of this element. He began by providing a detailed explanation of his remit and then evaluated the success of promotional and advertising campaigns, qualitatively, through focus group interviews with representatives from the extractive industry.

Ideas for evidence

- Extracts from reports relating to improving work activities.
- Details of monitoring methods and results.
- Explanations of timescales and their significance.

Your ideas for evidence

Description of evidence	Location of evidence	Opportunities for cross-referencing	Reflection and analysis

K&U links

Suggested reading for knowledge and understanding purposes:

Cole, G.A., *Management: Theory and Practice,* 5th edition, chapters 23, 24 and 25.

Mullins, L.J., *Management and Organisational Behaviour,* 4th edition, chapters 2, 8 and 15.

Needham, D. et al., *Business for Higher Awards,* chapters 10, 11 and 14.

Cross-referencing

Evidence and knowledge from this element could be used in any of the mandatory and optional units.

Element A4.1 Improve work activities

Performance Criterion

(c) *The information you gather on trends and developments is relevant, reliable and sufficient to identify potential improvements.*

You should explain how any internal and external trends and developments are identified and used to improve work activities.

Interpretation

⬛ How do you gather internal and external information regarding trends and developments that impact on the work activities in your area of management responsibility?

⬛ How do you check the information to ensure it is appropriate?

⬛ How is it used?

Candidate illustration

Event route
Val explained in her analysis that she was part of a national network within social services departments that circulated information on changes in legislation and best practice guidelines (see PC (a)). She evidenced specific items of information obtained from the network. She also included information that she had obtained from the Internet concerning changes in legislation that was used in the briefing report to senior managers.

Event route
Kieron continued to extract from the report originally referenced in PC (a). The nature of his information was mostly internal and obtained through discussion with other managers and peers. In addition, Kieron obtained external information from customers regarding desired delivery times.

Ideas for evidence

⬛ Examples of the information used.

⬛ Extracts from reports detailing and referencing sources of information.

Your ideas for evidence

Description of evidence	Location of evidence	Opportunities for cross-referencing	Reflection and analysis

K&U links

Cole, G.A., *Management: Theory and Practice,* 5th edition, chapters 23, 24 and 25.

Mullins, L.J., *Management and Organisational Behaviour,* 4th edition, chapters 2, 8 and 15.

Needham, D. et al., *Business for Higher Awards,* chapters 10, 11 and 14.

Cross-referencing

Evidence and knowledge from this element could be used in any of the mandatory and optional units.

Element A4.1 Improve work activities

Performance Criterion

(d) You present your recommendations for improvements in activities to relevant people at an appropriate time.

> To meet the requirements of this PC you will need to detail specific instances where you have presented these kinds of recommendations. Situations may include formal presentations, supervision sessions and team meetings. Explain your approach and why your presentation was timely. Again, relevant people must include at least two of the following: higher-level managers or sponsors, peers and specialists.

Interpretation

▉ Under what circumstances have you made these kinds of recommendations?

▉ Who else was involved?

▉ Why were the timescales appropriate?

Candidate illustration

Event route
Both Callum and Rosie were able to continue using their research and project reports as evidence here, highlighting the purpose of the reports and their specific remit, together with the conclusions and recommendation sections. Each clearly explained the relevance of their abstracts to the requirements of this PC in their reports. In addition, Rosie gave a brief presentation to managers based on her report prior to its distribution. She included her overhead transparencies from the presentation as additional evidence, explaining the timescales in her analysis.

Ideas for evidence

▉ Extracts from reports detailing recommendations.

▉ Plans for implementation of findings.

▉ Details of presentations given.

▉ Notes of conversations.

▉ Minutes of planning meetings.

Your ideas for evidence

Description of evidence	Location of evidence	Opportunities for cross-referencing	Reflection and analysis

K&U links   Suggested reading for knowledge and understanding purposes:

Cole, G.A., *Management: Theory and Practice*, 5th edition, chapters 23, 24 and 25.

Mullins, L.J., *Management and Organisational Behaviour*, 4th edition, chapters 2, 8 and 15.

Needham, D. et al., *Business for Higher Awards*, chapters 10, 11 and 14.

Cross-referencing   Evidence and knowledge from this element could be used in any of the mandatory and optional units.

Element A4.1 Improve work activities

Performance Criterion

(e) *You present your plans for implementing change to relevant people at an appropriate time, level and pace.*

> You may be able to link to PC (d) if your recommendations for improvements included changes in activities. Focus on the timescales and the way in which you pitched your presentation to suit the needs of those involved.

Interpretation

▮ How have you presented plans for change?

▮ Who was involved?

▮ Did your knowledge of those involved dictate the nature of your presentation?

Candidate illustration

Event route
Kieron and his project team (see PC (a)) met monthly with the project board, consisting of senior managers from all departments and external organisations involved. The purpose of the meeting was to provide information on progress against pre-planned timescales and achievements. Kieron included the minutes of the meeting and annotated the project report (previously submitted for PC (a)) to highlight areas of discussion. The project process was clearly explained in Kieron's analysis.

Event route
Callum continued to focus on the marketing report he was compiling (see PC (b)). The report, annotated at appropriate places, was submitted as evidence of presentation of plans. Callum also included a witness testimony from the marketing manager, confirming that distribution of the report was within the timescales agreed and that the report was appropriate for its purpose. Distribution lists were also included.

Ideas for evidence

▮ Cross-reference to existing evidence used in this element, if appropriate.

▮ Extracts from relevant reports, annotated to explain their relevance.

▮ Agendas and minutes from meetings where you have presented plans.

▮ Details of the plans themselves.

▮ Handouts and overhead transparencies used in presentations.

▮ Witness testimony from others involved.

▮ Details of the other people involved.

Your ideas for evidence

Description of evidence	Location of evidence	Opportunities for cross-referencing	Reflection and analysis

K&U links

Suggested reading for knowledge and understanding purposes:

Cole, G.A., *Management: Theory and Practice,* 5th edition, chapters 23, 24 and 25.

Mullins, L.J., *Management and Organisational Behaviour,* 4th edition, chapters 2, 8 and 15.

Needham, D. et al., *Business for Higher Awards,* chapters 10, 11 and 14.

Cross-referencing

Evidence and knowledge from this element could be used in any of the mandatory and optional units.

Element A4.1   Improve work activities

Performance Criterion

(f) You confirm relevant people's understanding of the implications of the change and their commitment to their role in it.

You may be able to link to PCs (d) and (e), if appropriate. Explain how you qualify others' understanding. This may have been actioned through discussion, supervision or question and answer sessions. Focus on how you sought and obtained the support and cooperation of others.

Interpretation

■ How do you confirm others' understanding of your proposals for improving work activities?

■ In what way have you explained implications?

■ How have you sought others' cooperation?

■ Have you given others the opportunity to clarify the implications and their role?

Candidate illustration

Event route
Rosie was able to cross-reference to evidence of a presentation given on her research into fundraising activities (see PC (d)). Her presentation included the opportunity for questions in a plenary session. In her analysis, Rosie explained that the presentation was designed to reinforce the issues detailed in the report and to assist others to identify their roles in maximising income generated from fundraising activities.

Event route
Val was able to cross-reference to the evidence submitted for PC (a) of this element. The team meetings held to discuss work activities affected by changes in legislation were used specifically to confirm her team's understanding of changes and to specify their roles. Val obtained a testimony from one of her team confirming the value of the meetings and what was gained from them.

Ideas for evidence

■ Cross-reference to existing evidence used in this element, if appropriate.

■ Details of interventions designed to brief and inform people of changes:
  – minutes of meetings;
  – reports;
  – presentations;
  – question and answer sessions;
  – written briefings;
  – discussion papers;
  – in-house bulletins and staff information.

Your ideas for evidence

Description of evidence	Location of evidence	Opportunities for cross-referencing	Reflection and analysis

K&U links

Suggested reading for knowledge and understanding purposes:

Cole, G.A., *Management: Theory and Practice*, 5th edition, chapters 23, 24 and 25.

Mullins, L.J., *Management and Organisational Behaviour*, 4th edition, chapters 2, 8 and 15.

Needham, D. et al., *Business for Higher Awards*, chapters 10, 11 and 14.

Cross-referencing

Evidence and knowledge from this element could be used in any of the mandatory and optional units.

Element A4.1   Improve work activities

Performance Criterion

(g) *Your monitoring of the change is significant to ensure the intended improvements are achieved.*

> You can link to previous evidence used throughout this element, if appropriate. Explain how you have compared planned changes to actual occurrences and their effect.

Interpretation

▪ How have you monitored changes to work activities?

▪ Have you ensured that methods of monitoring are appropriate?

▪ How have you acted on the outcomes of the monitoring to ensure that changes to work activities are achieved as planned?

Candidate illustration

Event route
Kieron continued to use his project work on improving delivery times (see PCs (a), (c) and (e)). Following implementation of its suggestions, the project group closely monitored delivery times by tracking orders from initial receipt through production and packaging to delivery. Trends were improving, but the team needed to reduce the time products were stored prior to distribution. Kieron included a detailed personal statement covering monitoring techniques and also submitted a subsequent report detailing the need for improvements in warehousing systems.

Event route
Having undertaken extensive research into the effectiveness of fundraising activities (see PCs (b), (d) and (f)), Rosie proposed that certain activities were dropped in favour of more cost-effective and profitable events. This was accepted and Rosie began monitoring income generation over a specified period of time to ensure that the strategy was increasing income. She cross-referenced to her research project and annotated the areas that detailed the events to be dropped and also included her proposals for monitoring income.

Ideas for evidence

▪ Cross-reference to existing evidence submitted for this element, if appropriate.

▪ Details of monitoring methods used.

▪ Outcomes of monitoring.

▪ Personal statement detailing action taken.

Your ideas for evidence

Description of evidence	Location of evidence	Opportunities for cross-referencing	Reflection and analysis

K&U links

Suggested reading for knowledge and understanding purposes:

Cole, G.A., *Management: Theory and Practice,* 5th edition, chapters 23, 24 and 25.

Mullins, L.J., *Management and Organisational Behaviour,* 4th edition, chapters 2, 8 and 15.

Needham, D. et al., *Business for Higher Awards,* chapters 10, 11 and 14.

Cross-referencing

Evidence and knowledge from this element could be used in any of the mandatory and optional units.

Element A4.1   Improve work activities

Performance Criterion	*(h) You report the results of the change to relevant people in the agreed format and timescale.*

> Explain how you keep others up to date regarding progress. Detail the circumstances and justify your methods of reporting and the timescales involved.

Interpretation

■ How are progress reports provided?

■ Who are the relevant people?

■ Why are methods of reporting and the timescales involved significant in your organisation?

Candidate illustration

Event route
Kieron was able to cross-reference to evidence submitted for PC (g). The report submitted was highlighted to illustrate results of changes and the further action required regarding storage and warehousing of products. Kieron also submitted a witness testimony from his line manager, the managing director, confirming that timescales had been updated and that the report was the most appropriate means of communicating results.

Event route
Rosie continued her theme of research into improvements in fundraising activities. Her report of results consisted mainly of calculations spread over time, demonstrating improvements in net funds raised by the charity due to a more cost-effective and efficient approach to fundraising activities. The report was discussed at a meeting with her team and line manager and forwarded to the charity board for information.

Ideas for evidence

■ Cross-reference to existing evidence used for this element, if appropriate.

■ Details of results of monitoring changes:
 – calculations;
 – reports;
 – briefing and information papers;
 – computerised printouts.

■ Minutes of meetings.

■ Witness testimony from others involved.

Your ideas for evidence

Description of evidence	Location of evidence	Opportunities for cross-referencing	Reflection and analysis

K&U links

Suggested reading for knowledge and understanding purposes:

Cole, G.A., *Management: Theory and Practice,* 5th edition, chapters 23, 24 and 25.

Mullins, L.J., *Management and Organisational Behaviour,* 4th edition, chapters 2, 8 and 15.

Needham, D. et al., *Business for Higher Awards,* chapters 10, 11 and 14.

Cross-referencing

Evidence and knowledge from this element could be used in any of the mandatory and optional units.

Element A4.1 Improve work activities

Performance Criterion

(i) *The quality of the work for which you are responsible continues to meet the agreed standard throughout the period of change.*

> Detail how you ensure that the quality of work activities undertaken is not compromised by change.

Interpretation

■ How is the standard of work agreed?

■ Is this dictated by your organisation, legislation, best practice guidelines or customer expectations?

■ Which methods do you use to ensure that standards of work are maintained?

■ What changes have taken place which may have threatened the quality of your work?

■ How did you manage the change?

Candidate illustration

Event route
Throughout the project (see PC (a) onwards), Kieron maintained his own work role and ensured that the sales team operated as before. He included details of supervision notes with staff, illustrating his continued support of them throughout the project. He also included a witness testimony from the managing director confirming that the standard of work in his team had not deteriorated due to the changes being made.

Event route
Val ensured that, despite amendments to working practices following changes in national legislation, all her team were verbally briefed and received written guidance on operating methods. This was submitted as evidence here. In addition, Val included some client information confirming that services were still being provided in accordance with existing organisational, legal and best practice requirements. She detailed this evidence in her analysis to ensure that her assessor understood its relevance.

Ideas for evidence

■ Supervision records.

■ Minutes of team meetings.

■ Briefing and information documents.

■ Written guidelines.

■ Client/customer/service user feedback.

■ Witness testimony from senior managers confirming maintained standards of work throughout the period of change.

Your ideas for evidence

Description of evidence	Location of evidence	Opportunities for cross-referencing	Reflection and analysis

K&U links

Suggested reading for knowledge and understanding purposes:

Cole, G.A., *Management: Theory and Practice,* 5th edition, chapters 23, 24 and 25.

Mullins, L.J., *Management and Organisational Behaviour,* 4th edition, chapters 2, 8 and 15.

Needham, D. et al., *Business for Higher Awards,* chapters 10, 11 and 14.

Cross-referencing

Evidence and knowledge from this element could be used in any of the mandatory and optional units.

| Element A4.2 | **Recommend improvements to organisational plans** |

Performance Criterion

(a) *Your recommendations for improvements to organisational plans are based on sufficient, valid and reliable information.*

> We recommend that you familiarise yourself with all the performance criteria for this element before beginning this PC. You will need to explain the circumstances and organisational context of the relevant organisational plans. Detail how your recommendations came about and the information used to justify them. Recommendations must be both of the spoken and written kind.

Interpretation

- Which organisational plans have you been involved with?
- What kinds of recommendations have you made?
- What were the circumstances?
- What kinds of information did you base your recommendations on?

Candidate illustration

Event route
Val drew on her contribution and involvement in the restructuring of her department. As part of a branch management team, Val had suggested improvements to the structure of the branch in order to assist staff in providing a higher standard and broader range of services to the general public. She based her recommendations on feedback from clients and staff collected throughout the previous year. Her recommendations in the form of a briefing document, together with examples of written feedback from service users and staff, were submitted as evidence.

Event route
Kieron drew on his work on organisational plans to expand market share by exporting to Europe (see Unit C2, Element C2.1, PC (e)). He cross-referenced to his report detailing options and recommendations. Both Val and Kieron obtained witness testimonies from their managers which confirmed how they also explained their recommendations, verbally, at relevant opportunities.

Ideas for evidence

- Cross-reference to existing evidence used for this NVQ, if appropriate.
- Examples of recommendations.
- Briefing papers.
- Minutes of meetings.
- Examples of the information used to formulate recommendations.

Your ideas for evidence

Description of evidence	Location of evidence	Opportunities for cross-referencing	Reflection and analysis

K&U links

Suggested reading for knowledge and understanding purposes:

Cole, G.A., *Management: Theory and Practice,* 5th edition, chapters 16, 17 and 18.

Mullins, L.J., *Management and Organisational Behaviour,* 4th edition, chapter 9.

Needham, D. et al., *Business for Higher Awards,* chapters 10, 11 and 14.

Cross-referencing

Evidence and knowledge from this element could be used in any of the mandatory and optional units.

Element A4.2 Recommend improvements to organisational plans

**Performance
Criterion**

*(b) Your recommendations support the achievement of the
organisation's mission, aims and objectives.*

> Link to previous performance criteria, if appropriate. Detail how you
> ensure that any recommendations for improvements are congruent
> with your organisation's plans. Explain the mission and relevant aims
> and objectives, and how they have informed your recommendations.

Interpretation

■ What is the mission of your organisation?

■ Which aims and objectives are relevant to your
recommendations?

■ How have you taken these into account when compiling your
recommendations for improvements to organisational plans?

**Candidate
illustration**

Event route
Val included her organisation's mission statement and her branch
aims and objectives for the coming year as background information.
She then annotated the report included in PC (a) to show how it was
congruent with her recommendations. She provided detailed analysis
of her evidence to make the link between these organisational
requirements and her recommendations.

Event route
Kieron had been given a specific remit by the managing director to
explore export opportunities in Europe. Kieron highlighted the remit
from the report submitted for PC (a) and annotated the relevant
sections of the report to explain how he had kept to the remit. Kieron
also obtained a witness testimony from the managing director
confirming his contribution to the advancement of organisational
plans.

Ideas for evidence

■ Cross-reference to existing evidence used for this NVQ, if
appropriate.

■ Extracts from reports, explaining their significance in terms of
organisational plans and objectives.

■ Details of presentations given.

■ Witness testimony from senior manager confirming your
contribution to the advancement of organisational plans and
objectives.

Your ideas for evidence

Description of evidence	Location of evidence	Opportunities for cross-referencing	Reflection and analysis

K&U links

Suggested reading for knowledge and understanding purposes:

Cole, G.A., *Management: Theory and Practice,* 5th edition, chapters 16, 17 and 18.

Mullins, L.J., *Management and Organisational Behaviour,* 4th edition, chapter 9.

Needham, D. et al., *Business for Higher Awards,* chapters 10, 11 and 14.

Cross-referencing

Evidence and knowledge from this element could be used in any of the mandatory and optional units.

Element A4.2 Recommend improvements to organisational plans

Performance Criterion

(c) You accurately identify and record the implications of the recommended changes.

> Link to previous performance criteria in this element, if appropriate. Explain how you justify your recommendations through identifying their effect on your area of work. Detail how these are recorded or planned for.

Interpretation

■ What are the implications of your recommendations?

■ Why is it important to identify the likely implications of recommendations?

■ How is this done?

Candidate illustration

Event route
Both Kieron and Val were able to continue using their respective reports, where their recommendations were justified and explained in full. They simply highlighted and annotated the relevant areas and gave a detailed analysis of the evidence.

Ideas for evidence

■ Extracts from reports or briefing documents identifying implications and justifying your recommendations.

■ Minutes of meetings.

■ Details of presentations given.

Your ideas for evidence

Description of evidence	Location of evidence	Opportunities for cross-referencing	Reflection and analysis

K&U links

Suggested reading for knowledge and understanding purposes:

Cole, G.A., *Management: Theory and Practice,* 5th edition, chapters 16, 17 and 18.

Mullins, L.J., *Management and Organisational Behaviour,* 4th edition, chapter 9.

Needham, D. et al., *Business for Higher Awards,* chapters 10, 11 and 14.

Cross-referencing

Evidence and knowledge from this element could be used in any of the mandatory and optional units.

Element A4.2   Recommend improvements to organisational plans

Performance Criterion

(d) *You clearly present your recommendations to the people in the organisation most likely to act on them.*

> Explain the circumstances behind your recommendations, justifying your method of presentation. Focus on the other people involved; how did you identify them as being the most relevant people to consider your recommendations? This may be because of relationships, responsibilities, seniority, span of control, and organisation structure and culture.

Interpretation

▌ How are your recommendations presented?

▌ Why is this method appropriate?

▌ Who is most likely to act on your recommendations for improvements to organisational plans?

▌ Why is this?

Candidate illustration

Event route
Kieron cross-referenced to where he had given a presentation to the managing director and departmental managers on the implications of the planned export advice. Handouts and overhead transparencies were used as evidence. In his analysis, Kieron explained the responsibilities of the people present and why they were key personnel in the export plans.

Event route
Val submitted her report to the branch management team, composed of peers and senior managers. She invited written feedback on her recommendations through a memo attached to the report. The memo, together with a personal statement explaining who the other people involved were and their significance, was submitted as evidence.

Ideas for evidence

▌ Cross-reference to existing evidence used in this element, if appropriate.

▌ Details of the other people involved.

▌ Minutes sent to those people.

▌ Details of the structure and personnel in your organisation.

Your ideas for evidence

Description of evidence	Location of evidence	Opportunities for cross-referencing	Reflection and analysis

K&U links	Suggested reading for knowledge and understanding purposes:
	Cole, G.A., *Management: Theory and Practice*, 5th edition, chapters 16, 17 and 18.
	Mullins, L.J., *Management and Organisational Behaviour*, 4th edition, chapter 9.
	Needham, D. et al., *Business for Higher Awards*, chapters 10, 11 and 14.
Cross-referencing	Evidence and knowledge from this element could be used in any of the mandatory and optional units.

Element A4.2 Recommend improvements to organisational plans

Performance Criterion

(e) *You handle the discussions relating to recommendations positively and constructively.*

> Discussions must be both one-to-one and during group meetings. Detail specific instances where your recommendations have been discussed. Explain how you have defended and advocated your recommendations during these discussions.

Interpretation

■ Where and in what circumstances have your recommendations for improvements to organisational plans been discussed?

■ Who else was involved?

■ How did you manage the discussion?

Candidate illustration

Event route
Val included the minutes of two branch management team meetings where discussions had occurred around her recommendations for the restructuring of the branch. She also included a personal statement explaining the minutes and her actions during the meetings.

Event route
Kieron was able to cross-reference to the presentation evidenced for PC (d). He had kept notes of the discussions and questions asked, and was able to include this as evidence. He also included a witness testimony from colleagues confirming that he handled discussions in a professional manner.

Ideas for evidence

■ Cross-reference to existing evidence used in this element, if appropriate.

■ Minutes of meetings where your recommendations were discussed.

■ Records of discussions(video, audio or written notes).

■ Witness testimony from those involved in the discussions.

Your ideas for evidence

Description of evidence	Location of evidence	Opportunities for cross-referencing	Reflection and analysis

K&U links

Suggested reading for knowledge and understanding purposes:

Cole, G.A., *Management: Theory and Practice,* 5th edition, chapters 16, 17 and 18.

Mullins, L.J., *Management and Organisational Behaviour,* 4th edition, chapter 9.

Needham, D. et al., *Business for Higher Awards,* chapters 10, 11 and 14.

Cross-referencing

Evidence and knowledge from this element could be used in any of the mandatory and optional units.

CHAPTER 6

Unit C2 — Develop your own resources

Element C2.1   Develop yourself to improve your performance

Performance Criterion

(a) *You assess your performance and identify your development needs at appropriate intervals.*

> This PC requires you to explain the assessment processes (formal or informal) that you use. To complete this PC successfully you will need to show that you objectively assess your own performance. In addition, you will need to show how you identify your own development needs. Make sure you detail these development needs and explain their significance. Finally, your evidence should demonstrate that your self-assessment is not a one-off occurrence.

Interpretation

- What indicators do you use to judge your performance?
- What form does the assessment take?
- What is the outcome of the assessment?
- How are your assessments used to identify development needs?
- How do assessment timescales impact on your work role?

Candidate illustration

Val utilised her experiences with self-appraisal, since assessment of this nature routinely takes place in her organisation using centrally administered documentation. In her case, completing this PC was merely a matter of photocopying this evidence and putting it forward for assessment, as development needs were already linked to her organisation's training needs analysis process.

Kieron's company does not have formal procedures for self-assessment and development. Kieron therefore joined up with other managers progressing their NVQ and together they set up their own continuous professional development (CPD) files to enable them to monitor and evaluate their own development. Flow charts, knowledge maps and training events formed part of his evidence. He supplemented these with witness testimonies from other members of the CPD group. Kieron's main development area, in terms of skills, was to improve his team working.

Ideas for evidence

- Flow chart or mind-map diagrams detailing the self-assessment process.
- Outcomes of formal two-way appraisal and supervision.
- Completed documentation.
- Personal action plans.
- Extracts from CPD files.

Your ideas for evidence

Description of evidence	Location of evidence	Opportunities for cross-referencing	Reflection and analysis

K&U links

Suggested reading for knowledge and understanding purposes:

Cole, G.A., *Management: Theory and Practice,* 5th edition, chapters 27 and 44.

Mullins, L.J., *Management and Organisational Behaviour,* 4th edition, chapter 4, pp. 120–9, chapters 8, 15 and 21.

Needham, D. et al., *Business for Higher Awards,* chapters 10, 11, 25, 26, 27 and 28.

Cross-referencing

Evidence and knowledge from this element can be used in the following mandatory units of NVQ Management Level 4: **A4**, **C5**, **B2**, **C2**; and the following optional units: **C10**, **C13**, **C15**, **F2**, **F4**, **F6**, **F7**.

Element C2.1 Develop yourself to improve your performance

Performance Criterion

(b) Your assessment is based on your current objectives and likely future requirements.

> To meet the requirements of this PC you will have to focus on your current and planned personal performance objectives and explain their nature and significance. Make sure you fully detail the part of the assessment process that illustrates the incorporation of work-based objectives.

Interpretation

■ What are your current personal performance objectives?

■ How are these fed into your assessment process?

■ How are likely future requirements identified?

■ Who else is involved?

■ How is assessment planned to take the above into account?

Candidate illustration

Event route

Val drew evidence from completed organisational documentation relating to supervision records and appraisal outcomes. Current objectives and future requirements were included in her contribution to the management team's business plan, and detailed in a report sent to her head of department. Extracts from the report were highlighted and submitted as evidence, and were linked back to her supervision records and appraisal outcomes.

As a trainee manager, Callum found this PC challenging. His approach was to incorporate his objectives relating to personal effectiveness, time management and delegation skills into his CPD portfolio, from which he extracted his evidence. This included both his and his line manager's qualitative rating of his own performance against predetermined criteria, and actions that needed to be taken as a result of the exercise.

Ideas for evidence

■ Outcomes of formal two-way supervision and appraisal.

■ Extracts from CPD files.

■ Completed documentation relating to management development and competence.

■ Personal action plans.

■ Extracts from relevant reports.

Your ideas for evidence

Description of evidence	Location of evidence	Opportunities for cross-referencing	Reflection and analysis

K&U links

Suggested reading for knowledge and understanding purposes:

Cole, G.A., *Management: Theory and Practice,* 5th edition, chapters 27 and 44.

Mullins, L.J., *Management and Organisational Behaviour,* 4th edition, chapter 4, pp. 120–9, chapters 8, 15 and 21.

Needham, D. et al., *Business for Higher Awards,* chapters 10, 11, 25, 26, 27 and 28.

Cross-referencing

Evidence and knowledge from this element can be used in the following mandatory units of NVQ Management Level 4: **A4, C5, B2, C2**; and the following optional units: **C10, C13, C15, F2, F4, F6, F7**.

Element C2.1 Develop yourself to improve your performance

Performance Criterion

(c) Your assessment takes account of the skills you need to work effectively with other team members.

> It is helpful first to define your role in your chosen team. Focus on this team and explain the key skills you need in order to work effectively with your fellow team members. It will be useful for your assessor if you indicate the team's remit, background and purpose. Illustrate that part of your personal performance assessment process that allows for a team-working skills audit, with examples and an explanation of their significance.

Interpretation

- Link to the previous PCs, if appropriate.
- What team-working skills do you need?
- Do your development needs, current objectives and likely future requirements include team-working skills?
- Who are the other team members?
- How do they indicate the skills that they need?
- How does your skill in working with others impact on your ability to work as part of a team?
- Does your organisation specify core team-working skills?

Candidate illustration

Event route
Rosie focused on her ability to manage volunteers. Of primary importance both to her role as a manager and to achieving the organisation's goals is the recruitment, work allocation and retention of committed volunteers. Working with teams of volunteers, any skills gaps she may have had were identified through self-analysis frameworks and management training course materials, and were fed into action planning for personal development. Examples of completed self-analysis and personal development documentation were submitted as evidence.

Kieron again drew from his CPD file, as he found that evidence presented itself as part of the process he had detailed earlier in the element (see PC (a)). As Kieron's team was spread over several sites in the area, his focus was on communication, team building and time management.

Ideas for evidence

See PCs (a) and (b).

- Completed personal analysis frameworks, such as the Belbin team traits analysis document.

■ Team cohesiveness analysis (Tuckman, 1965, referenced in Cole, *Management: Theory and Practice,* 4th edition, chapter 12, 'Teams at Work').

■ Details of how the need for team-working skills are identified:
  – completed self-analysis frameworks;
  – completed appraisal documentation;
  – supervision outcomes;
  – personal action plans.

■ Witness testimony from an appropriate person, e.g. a team member, colleague, mentor, line manager or training officer.

Your ideas for evidence

Description of evidence	Location of evidence	Opportunities for cross-referencing	Reflection and analysis

K&U links

Suggested reading for knowledge and understanding purposes: Cole, G.A., *Management: Theory and Practice,* 5th edition, chapters 27 and 44.

Mullins, L.J., *Management and Organisational Behaviour,* 4th edition, chapter 4, pp. 120–9, chapters 8, 15 and 21.

Needham, D. et al., *Business for Higher Awards,* chapters 10, 11, 25, 26, 27 and 28.

Cross-referencing

Evidence and knowledge from this element can be used in the following mandatory units of NVQ Management Level 4: **A4**, **C5**, **B2**, **C2**; and the following optional units: **C10**, **C13**, **C15**, **F2**, **F4**, **F6**, **F7**.

Element C2.1   Develop yourself to improve your performance

Performance Criterion

(d) Your plans for personal development are consistent with the needs you have identified and the resources available.

> You will need to explain how you match your identified needs to specific planned development activities, such as job shadowing, training, distance learning, external courses, tests and other experiences. Detail the resources available to you at work and those you have obtained independently.

Interpretation

- Link to the evidence submitted for previous PCs, if appropriate.
- What are your plans for personal development? Are they formalised?
- How are your development needs represented (standard format, action plans, supervision records)?
- Are the desired resources identified?
- Do they correspond with what is available to you?

Candidate illustration

Val cross-referenced to the completion of personal and team training needs analysis documentation. This had to be submitted to the staff development section as a way of identifying needs and means of meeting them. Val's personal development needs focused on time management and assertiveness skills. To meet this need she applied for places on the corresponding corporate courses.

Kieron detailed his personal development needs, methods of meeting them and projected costs in a briefing document sent to the director. In the report, he proposed using a small part of his budget to attend a regional training event, organised by the local Business Link organisation. The event examined the practical, financial and legal implications of exporting within the European Union (EU), and corresponded with Kieron's new assignment as sales manager since part of his remit was to take advantage of the reduction in EU barriers to trade.

Ideas for evidence

- Training needs analysis documentation.
- Personal statement detailing avenues for personal development within your organisation.
- Reports to decision makers detailing plans for personal development.
- Correspondence between you and internal/external training providers.

Your ideas for evidence

Description of evidence	Location of evidence	Opportunities for cross-referencing	Reflection and analysis

K&U links

Suggested reading for knowledge and understanding purposes:

Cole, G.A., *Management: Theory and Practice,* 5th edition, chapters 27 and 44.

Mullins, L.J., *Management and Organisational Behaviour,* 4th edition, chapter 4, pp. 120–9, chapters 8, 15 and 21.

Needham, D. et al., *Business for Higher Awards,* chapters 10, 11, 25, 26, 27 and 28.

Cross-referencing

Evidence and knowledge from this element can be used in the following mandatory units of NVQ Management Level 4: **A4, C5, B2, C2**; and the following optional units: **C10, C13, C15, F2, F4, F6, F7**.

Element C2.1   Develop yourself to improve your performance

Performance Criterion

(e) Your plans for personal development contain specific, measurable, realistic and challenging objectives.

> This PC requires you to explain how you arrive at suitable objectives for personal development. It may be difficult to find actual performance evidence in support of this, but you should, in any case, explain those factors that impact on the nature of your personal development plans, for example: availability of resources, time, finance, organisational culture, procedures and policy, line manager involvement, your authority to make decisions, etc. In doing this you will be able to explain how you ensure that personal development plans are SMART (**s**pecific, **m**easurable, **a**chievable, **r**ealistic and **t**ime-specific) and challenging. Illustrate how you finalised plans, for example discussions with relevant people, cost–benefit analysis, considering likely opportunity cost, synthesis of information.

Interpretation

Link to previous PCs, if appropriate.

▪ Once you have identified personal development needs, how do you break them down into objectives?

▪ Is this done in a systematic way or on a situational, needs-led basis?

▪ How do you tailor these objectives to ensure that, in achieving them, you will have undergone the personal development as identified?

▪ Who else is involved?

▪ How do you ensure that your personal development needs are SMART and challenging?

Candidate illustration

Val cross-referenced to her completed training needs analysis documentation. This allowed her to identify development needs against a series of factors particular to her organisation. She justified these actions in her analysis by linking training needs to the mission statement, vision, core values, departmental plans and team objectives within her organisation. In doing this, she was able to demonstrate clearly that she had based her plans on her personal needs and on the values and requirements of her organisation. This ensured that plans were specific and outcomes-based. In addition, the nature of the training needs analysis documentation meant that the plans were measurable. Finally, she supplemented her performance evidence with a personal statement which explained why they were challenging.

Kieron obtained the literature for his course on exporting from Business Link and wrote a report to the director of his organisation requesting financial support and time off to attend the course. He used this PC to structure his report, ensuring that it covered all the requirements. As a result, he wrote a very persuasive report and his manager duly agreed to support him!

Ideas for evidence

▋ Flow chart or mind map incorporating a personal statement to explain thought and decision-making processes and the factors that impact on them.

▋ Details of personal development plans in the form of reports, briefing documents, completed training needs analysis documentation.

▋ Correspondence with relevant people: trainers, colleagues, line managers, mentors and external organisations.

▋ Evidence cross-referenced from previous PCs where appropriate.

Your ideas for evidence

Description of evidence	Location of evidence	Opportunities for cross-referencing	Reflection and analysis

K&U links

Suggested reading for knowledge and understanding purposes:

Cole, G.A., *Management: Theory and Practice,* 5th edition, chapters 27 and 44.

Mullins, L.J., *Management and Organisational Behaviour,* 4th edition, chapter 4, pp. 120–9, chapters 8, 15 and 21.

Needham, D. et al., *Business for Higher Awards,* chapters 10, 11, 25, 26, 27 and 28.

Cross-referencing

Evidence and knowledge from this element can be used in the following mandatory units of NVQ Management Level 4: **A4, C5, B2, C2**; and the following optional units: **C10, C13, C15, F2, F4, F6, F7**.

| *Element* **C2.1** | # Develop yourself to improve your performance |

Performance Criterion

(f) You obtain support from relevant people to help you to create learning opportunities.

A good way to start this PC is to examine the network of support available to you. Detail how you draw support from this network in order to create learning opportunities. These opportunities need not be high profile or involve direct training events. They may involve job shadowing, increased responsibility, job rotation, reading, sharing ideas through brainstorming, research and reflection. Explain who else is involved in the learning opportunities and illustrate how you have sought support from them.

Interpretation

- What kinds of support are needed?
- Why is support needed?
- Who are the relevant people able to offer support?
- Is this support given in a formal or informal way?
- How do these people assist you in creating learning opportunities?
- Are relevant people determined by the nature of the identified personal development need?

Candidate illustration

Callum relied heavily on his line manager to assist him in creating learning opportunities. As well as being part of the in-house management development programme, Callum was also still involved in an induction programme designed to give participants an insight into the workings of each department within his organisation. Callum was responsible for making initial contact with key personnel to arrange visits and to attend team meetings. He used correspondence from key people, explaining in a personal statement who they were and the significance of the meetings. Arrangements and events were recorded in Callum's induction handbook, which he also used as evidence.

Rosie made reference to contacts made with the general public and those responsible for authorising development opportunities within her organisation. Her learning opportunities related to obtaining quantitative and qualitative data and information from the general public regarding the nature of service provided by her team. She used this information to analyse her management of the team and the project they were working on. The analysis was then used as the basis for a development plan to assist Rosie in recruiting and developing volunteer workers. Finally, an action plan was presented to senior management and discussed to identify cost-effective and relevant personal learning opportunities.

Ideas for evidence

◼ Details of the individuals involved and how they were appropriate to development plans and the required learning opportunities.

◼ This can be evidenced through correspondence sent and received, and personal statements and witness testimonies from those involved.

◼ Development plans can also be included, highlighting and explaining areas that have been influenced by appropriate people.

Your ideas for evidence

Description of evidence	Location of evidence	Opportunities for cross-referencing	Reflection and analysis

K&U links

Suggested reading for knowledge and understanding purposes:

Cole, G.A., *Management: Theory and Practice,* 5th edition, chapters 27 and 44.

Mullins, L.J., *Management and Organisational Behaviour,* 4th edition, chapter 4, pp. 120–9, chapters 8, 15 and 21.

Needham, D. et al., *Business for Higher Awards,* chapters 10, 11, 25, 26, 27 and 28.

Cross-referencing

Evidence and knowledge from this element can be used in the following mandatory units of NVQ Management Level 4: **A4, C5, B2, C2**; and the following optional units: **C10, C13, C15, F2, F4, F6, F7.**

Develop yourself to improve your performance

Performance Criterion

(g) *You undertake development activities which are consistent with your plans for personal development.*

> The existence of written, approved development plans cannot clearly indicate the experiences inherent in actually undertaking development activities. You need to prove that you have carried out the activities as planned and that they were actually supportive in advancing your personal development. Focus on the activities and the work undertaken in several of them. Clearly evidence and explain how these activities met your development needs.

Interpretation

- Were your development plans put into action?
- How did this happen?
- Were the actions taken effective?

Candidate illustration

Callum continued using the evidence identified for PC (f), and followed the process through to attending meetings and visits at the various sites and departments within his organisation. He was required to keep notes of what had been learnt in an induction diary supplied on his first day. Photocopied extracts from the diary and the minutes from the meeting he attended were used as evidence and supported with a personal statement and two witness testimonies from others involved.

Rosie included a small amount of the data and information collected during her research (see PC (f)) and linked that to her need for knowledge of customers' perceptions of service provision. The checklist used when interviewing people was also included.

Ideas for evidence

- Diary extracts.
- Attendance lists from courses.
- Completed paper-based development activities.
- Videotaped evidence.
- Audiotaped evidence.
- All the above can be cross-referenced to plans and identified needs used for previous PCs in this element.

Your ideas for evidence

Description of evidence	Location of evidence	Opportunities for cross-referencing	Reflection and analysis

K&U links

Suggested reading for knowledge and understanding purposes:

Cole, G.A., *Management: Theory and Practice,* 5th edition, chapters 27 and 44.

Mullins, L.J., *Management and Organisational Behaviour,* 4th edition, chapter 4, pp. 120–9, chapters 8, 15 and 21.

Needham, D. et al., *Business for Higher Awards,* chapters 10, 11, 25, 26, 27 and 28.

Cross-referencing

Evidence and knowledge from this element can be used in the following mandatory units of NVQ Management Level 4: **A4**, **C5**, **B2**, **C2**; and the following optional units: **C10**, **C13**, **C15**, **F2**, **F4**, **F6**, **F7**.

Element C2.1

Develop yourself to improve your performance

Performance Criterion

(h) You obtain feedback from relevant people and use it to enhance your performance in the future.

> To meet the requirements of this PC you will need to focus clearly on performance feedback and the people who provide it. Link examples back to what you have already included as evidence for this element, for example identified training need and development plans. Explain how the feedback has confirmed or disconfirmed your perceptions of the benefits gained from the development activities. As a result of this information, detail the actions taken (or to be taken) that will further develop your performance as a manager.

Interpretation

- Do you actively seek feedback from relevant people?

- What form does feedback take?

- When is feedback sought?

- How do you use feedback to inform constructively on your personal progress?

Candidate illustration

On completing the time management course detailed in PC (d), Val set about putting her learning and knowledge into action. This involved prioritising tasks and a more defined focus on process issues, the delegation of work and personal effectiveness. To monitor her performance, she asked her staff and her line manager to inform her, on an ongoing basis, of how they thought she was doing. This information was given both verbally and in writing, at predetermined times. Val used the information to make informal improvements to her methods of operation.

Kieron's informal network of continuous professional development enthusiasts met weekly to exchange files, ideas and information. Kieron took the time and opportunity to request feedback on his approach to managing the exporting side of the organisation and was able to learn from the views of the group. This was then evidenced through notes taken and testimony from other group members.

Ideas for evidence

- Examples of written requests for feedback sent to appropriate people: memos, letters, email.

- Replies from these people.

- Examples of feedback received – either videotaped or audiotaped.

- Examples of changes made to personal practices .

Your ideas for evidence

Description of evidence	Location of evidence	Opportunities for cross-referencing	Reflection and analysis

K&U links Suggested reading for knowledge and understanding purposes:

Cole, G.A., *Management: Theory and Practice*, 5th edition, chapters 27 and 44.

Mullins, L.J., *Management and Organisational Behaviour*, 4th edition, chapter 4, pp. 120–9, chapters 8, 15 and 21.

Needham, D. et al., *Business for Higher Awards*, chapters 10, 11, 25, 26, 27 and 28.

Cross-referencing Evidence and knowledge from this element can be used in the following mandatory units of NVQ Management Level 4: **A4, C5, B2, C2**; and the following optional units: **C10, C13, C15, F2, F4, F6, F7**.

| Element C2.1 | Develop yourself to improve your performance |

Performance Criterion

(i) You update your plans for personal development at appropriate intervals.

As part of the personal performance management process, the review and updating of plans is essential to ensure continuous development. It also allows you to reflect on what has occurred and what has to happen in the future. Focus your analysis on the factors that influence the updating of plans, for example: feedback from the appropriate people, timescales, budgetary considerations, personal and organisational development needs. Detail what has been learnt and the nature of any updates based on impending work schedules, targets and milestones, and the skills within the team that you manage. Explain the updating process, the timescales involved and their significance.

Interpretation

▌ How are plans updated?

▌ Does this occur systematically?

▌ What processes and events influence the intervals between review times?

Candidate illustration

On completing the organisational awareness part of his induction, Callum attended a progress review interview with his head of department, which used personal one-to-one appraisal. The outcomes of the appraisal were documented and used to inform the next stage of Callum's management development programme. Copies of the completed appraisal documents and an explanation of the interview were included as evidence.

The results of the general research undertaken by Rosie were used as a basis for improving her team effectiveness, both internally and at the customer interface. The nature of the improvements included availability of information to the public, response times to queries, corporate image, fundraising activities and quality of service provision. Rosie took three core areas and planned personal and team development events around them, detailing proposals and justifications in a report to the regional manager. The report was highlighted in appropriate areas and used as evidence for the PC.

Ideas for evidence

▌ Updated personal action plans.

▌ Extracts from personal development portfolios.

▌ Relevant reports, memos or letters sent to appropriate people.

▌ Details of proposed future development activities.

▌ A personal statement explaining any or all of the above.

Your ideas for evidence

Description of evidence	Location of evidence	Opportunities for cross-referencing	Reflection and analysis

K&U links

Suggested reading for knowledge and understanding purposes:

Cole, G.A., *Management: Theory and Practice,* 5th edition, chapters 27 and 44.

Mullins, L.J., *Management and Organisational Behaviour,* 4th edition, chapter 4, pp. 120–9, chapters 8, 15 and 21.

Needham, D. et al., *Business for Higher Awards,* chapters 10, 11, 25, 26, 27 and 28.

Cross-referencing

Evidence and knowledge from this element can be used in the following mandatory units of NVQ Management Level 4: **A4**, **C5**, **B2**, **C2**; and the following optional units: **C10**, **C13**, **C15**, **F2**, **F4**, **F6**, **F7**.

Manage your own time and resources to meet your objectives

Performance Criterion

(a) *Your objectives are specific, measurable and achievable within organisational constraints.*

> This PC requires you to detail your personal objective-setting process. You may want to use a flow chart as evidence to show the factors that impact on this process. It's also important to explain the significance of each factor as it presents itself. Make sure your objectives are achievable. One way to meet the requirements of this PC would be to illustrate an incident where you have planned to achieve an objective by minimising the constraints on it.

Interpretation

- How do you set work objectives?
- Which criteria are used in setting them?
- How do you ensure that they are achievable?
- How do you identify likely constraints?
- In what ways do you make allowances for constraints?

Candidate illustration

Rosie focused on her team's objectives for the coming year. She realised that while general objectives for her area of work were written in business plans and promotional material, they had not been applied to her team and the allocation of responsibility. She set about doing this through a workshop with her team of volunteers. The workshop programme and outcomes were transcribed from flip charts and used as evidence, along with supporting testimonies from two team members.

Kieron focused on the work objectives associated with the export drive he was managing. He used extracts from supervision records of his sales team, highlighting and explaining how his allocated objectives linked to those of the sales team. Kieron emphasised the situational factors that were likely to impact on his objectives: time; lack of experience of the new European marketplace; competitors' products; the economic situation within the EU; and the ability of the production team to meet the projected increase in demand for products.

Ideas for evidence

- Details of how objectives are set; personal statement, team development sessions, planning documents.
- Flow chart detailing your personal objective-setting process and showing factors likely to impact on their achievement.
- Extracts from supervision documents where objectives have been put into operation through delegating responsibility.
- Witness testimony from those involved in the objective-setting process.
- Staff work schedules linked to objectives.

Your ideas for evidence

Description of evidence	Location of evidence	Opportunities for cross-referencing	Reflection and analysis

K&U links

Suggested reading for knowledge and understanding purposes:

Cole, G.A., *Management: Theory and Practice*, 5th edition, chapter 27.

Mullins, L.J., *Management and Organisational Behaviour*, 4th edition, chapter 13, pp. 458–65.

Needham, D. et al., *Business for Higher Awards*, chapters 10, 11, 25, 26, 27 and 28.

Cross-referencing

Evidence and knowledge from this element can be used in the following mandatory units of NVQ Management Level 4: **A2**, **A4**, **C5**, **D4**, **B2**, **B3**; and the following optional units: **C10**, **C13**, **C15**, **G1**.

Element C2.2 | # Manage your own time and resources to meet your objectives

Performance Criterion

(b) *You prioritise your objectives in line with organisational objectives and policies.*

To meet the requirements of this PC, you should give an insight into your organisation's key objectives and how they have been translated into your objectives. Detail the relationship between the two in order to explain how your own objectives are prioritised. If you employ any systematic method of prioritisation, explain it. Explain how you gather information to assist in prioritising objectives and the nature of that information.

Interpretation

- Link to the objectives detailed in PC (a).
- How are objectives prioritised?
- How are they linked to the wider objectives of your organisation?
- Which has an impact on the importance of your objectives?

Candidate illustration

Callum used appraisal and evaluation documentation as evidence for this PC. As a trainee manager, part of his programme involved identifying and prioritising personal objectives. His justification for the priorities had to be made verbally during an evaluation with his line manager. In preparation for the NVQ, Callum had the evaluation tape-recorded and was able to use the cassette as evidence in addition to the paper documents submitted.

Val continued to use the evidence included for Element C2.1, particularly PC (b). In addition, Val chaired a meeting with her team to action plan a document of objectives and delegate specific tasks to individuals. She linked this action plan to the business plan for her department in the reflection and analysis section of the NVQ, clearly demonstrating that she had met the national standard.

Ideas for evidence

- Use existing evidence for previous units and from Element C2.1.
- Appraisal and evaluation documentation.
- Audiotaped conversations.
- Videotaped meetings, planning events and workshops with your team.
- Organisation's business plan (highlighting your contribution).
- Local team action plans (stating relationship with business plan).

Your ideas for evidence

Description of evidence	Location of evidence	Opportunities for cross-referencing	Reflection and analysis

K&U links   Suggested reading for knowledge and understanding purposes:

Cole, G.A., *Management: Theory and Practice,* 5th edition, chapter 27.

Mullins, L.J., *Management and Organisational Behaviour,* 4th edition, chapter 13, pp. 458–65.

Needham, D. et al., *Business for Higher Awards,* chapters 10, 11, 25, 26, 27 and 28.

Cross-referencing   Evidence and knowledge from this element can be used in the following mandatory units of NVQ Management Level 4: **A2, A4, C5, D4, B2, B3**; and the following optional units: **C10, C13, C15, G1.**

Element C2.2 Manage your own time and resources to meet your objectives

Performance Criterion

(c) You plan your work activities so that they are consistent with your objectives and your personal resources.

> Once again, draw on evidence already included for this unit. Emphasise how you operationalise objectives through planning your own work programme. Detail the personal resources available or unavailable, for example: time, budgets, buildings, technology, people, authority, span of control and materials. Explain how these resources impact on your ability to complete personal work programmes.

Interpretation

▌ Do you use objectives to set your own work programmes?

▌ How do you do this?

▌ Who else is involved?

▌ What personal resources are available?

▌ How do personal resources impact on your ability to undertake work activities?

Candidate illustration

Working in the voluntary sector often requires fundraising in order to achieve objectives. Part of Rosie's role was to plan fundraising activities against prioritised objectives for the year. She used her timetabled plans and financial calculations to illustrate the need for work objectives to be linked to actual activities in order to ensure that her goals were achieved.

Kieron continued his focus on the drive to establish export links in the EU. Work objectives were linked to increasing overseas sales. He detailed these objectives in a presentation to his sales force, who included the accounts manager and sales representatives. The presentation format and overhead transparencies were submitted as evidence, along with a testimony from Kieron's line manager explaining how these objectives were linked to Kieron's personal development.

Ideas for evidence

▌ Cross-reference to existing evidence from previous units and from Element C2.1.

▌ Work programmes.

▌ Financial calculations.

▌ Materials from presentations.

▌ Witness testimony from appropriate people.

▌ Reports.

▌ Minutes of meetings.

■ Memos.

■ Email.

■ Letters.

Your ideas for evidence

Description of evidence	Location of evidence	Opportunities for cross-referencing	Reflection and analysis

K&U links

Suggested reading for knowledge and understanding purposes:

Cole, G.A., *Management: Theory and Practice,* 5th edition, chapter 27.

Mullins, L.J., *Management and Organisational Behaviour,* 4th edition, chapter 13, pp. 458–65.

Needham, D. et al., *Business for Higher Awards,* chapters 10, 11, 25, 26, 27 and 28.

Cross-referencing

Evidence and knowledge from this element can be used in the following mandatory units of NVQ Management Level 4: **A2, A4, C5, D4, B2, B3**; and the following optional units: **C10, C13, C15, G1**.

Manage your own time and resources to meet your objectives

Performance Criterion

(d) Your estimates of the time you need for activities are realistic and allow for unforeseen circumstances.

The evidence you put forward in support of this PC should clearly detail how you plan timescales and ensure that they are as accurate as possible. You should explain how you employ the principles of time management in assisting you to plan effectively. In addition, it will be necessary to illustrate your approach using examples from the workplace. Finally, make sure you explain the factors that may cause delay and how you have allowed for them in your calculations.

Interpretation

■ Link to previous evidence, if appropriate.

■ Do your plans contain timescales?

■ How are these calculated?

■ Which factors impact on these timescales?

■ Do you allow for these?

■ How are timescales represented in your plans?

Candidate illustration

Callum cross-referenced to evidence gained from his appraisal and evaluation documentation. This evidence evaluated areas such as time management skills, forward planning and managing non-routine occurrences. In his analysis, Callum detailed and explained the comments made by his manager and the circumstances in which his time management skills were utilised.

Val drew from a different part of her contribution to her department's business plan. This was highlighted and labelled to distinguish it from any other parts of the document already referenced. The evidence detailed timescales for the achievement of particular objectives, headed by the title 'Key milestones'. Likely delays were also highlighted and explained in terms of the need for policy statements, likely sickness and absence figures, details of staff turnover and the need to recruit staff in the coming year.

Ideas for evidence

■ Use existing evidence from previous units.

■ Appraisal and supervision documentation.

■ Team/section/departmental business plans.

■ Other planning documents.

■ Calculations relating to likely delays or non-routine events:
- budgetary considerations;
- staff turnover;
- sickness and absenteeism;
- resource allocation;
- reasonability.

Your ideas for evidence

Description of evidence	Location of evidence	Opportunities for cross-referencing	Reflection and analysis

K&U links

Suggested reading for knowledge and understanding purposes:

Cole, G.A., *Management: Theory and Practice,* 5th edition, chapter 27.

Mullins, L.J., *Management and Organisational Behaviour,* 4th edition, chapter 13, pp. 458–65.

Needham, D. et al., *Business for Higher Awards,* chapters 10, 11, 25, 26, 27 and 28.

Cross-referencing

Evidence and knowledge from this element can be used in the following mandatory units of NVQ Management Level 4: **A2**, **A4**, **C5**, **D4**, **B2**, **B3**; and the following optional units: **C10**, **C13**, **C15**, **G1**.

Element C2.2 Manage your own time and resources to meet your objectives

Performance Criterion

(e) *You delegate work to others in a way which makes the most efficient use of available time and resources.*

> This PC will require you to focus on events where you have delegated to members of your staff, colleagues and people outside your organisation. Detail the circumstances and the factors that determined the linking of people to the work to be delegated. Explain the process of reviewing activities against planned timescales, and the efficient use of the resources involved. Bear in mind that events can be routine or non-routine.

Interpretation

▮ Link to previous evidence, if appropriate.

▮ How do you identify work that can be delegated?

▮ How do you identify the most appropriate person or people to delegate to?

▮ Do you monitor progress of delegated activities?

▮ What criteria do you use to monitor progress?

▮ How is progress monitored and evaluated regarding timescales and the efficient use of the resources involved?

Candidate illustration

Rosie drew from the planning meeting she had evidenced for PC (a) of this element. The minutes of the planning meeting detailed delegated tasks and areas of responsibility for each team member. Rosie explained the decisions behind the delegation process in a personal statement and cross-referenced to the two testimonies already included in the evidence used for PC (a). Her decisions were based on the expertise and skills of individual team members, their existing workloads, and the priorities for the year detailed in the departmental business plan. Monitoring of progress was evidenced using extracts from supervision sessions held with a cross-section of team members.

Continuing the export sales drive event, Kieron detailed how he drew on the previous experience of members of his sales force to inform on where to delegate responsibility. Through discussion with colleagues and his sales force, he found that several members of the team had worked across Europe in previous jobs. He requested notes from each of them detailing what they had done and where, and from this information he was able to allocate tasks and responsibilities based on his plans and the experiences of the team. The notes were evidenced, along with extracts from the export strategy plan.

Ideas for evidence
- Use existing evidence from previous units.
- Planning documentation.
- Minutes of meetings where delegation occurred.
- Supervision documentation.
- Witness testimony.
- Personal statement.
- Notes and information used to inform decisions on delegation.

Your ideas for evidence

Description of evidence	Location of evidence	Opportunities for cross-referencing	Reflection and analysis

K&U links

Suggested reading for knowledge and understanding purposes:

Cole, G.A., *Management: Theory and Practice*, 5th edition, chapter 27.

Mullins, L.J., *Management and Organisational Behaviour*, 4th edition, chapter 13, pp. 458–65.

Needham, D. et al., *Business for Higher Awards*, chapters 10, 11, 25, 26, 27 and 28.

Cross-referencing

Evidence and knowledge from this element can be used in the following mandatory units of NVQ Management Level 4: **A2, A4, C5, D4, B2, B3**; and the following optional units: **C10, C13, C15, G1**.

Element C2.2   Manage your own time and resources to meet your objectives

Performance Criterion

(f) You take decisions as soon as you have sufficient information.

You will need to identify specific occurrences at work that required you to gather and use information to aid decision making. In your analysis, explain how information was gathered, checked for validity and used. Explain the circumstances and the implications of the decisions to be made. Focus on and detail the information used and the timescales involved.

Interpretation

■ When preparing to make decisions, how do you assess the amount of information that will be needed?

■ How do you gather and assess information?

■ How much time do you allow for this process?

■ How do you use the information to aid the decision-making process?

Candidate illustration

Kieron cross-referenced to the evidence used for PC (e). The notes from his sales force regarding their previous overseas work experience detailed the information gathered and used. Decisions made concerning the allocation of responsibility were based on this information. Kieron added a personal statement indicating the timescales involved and their significance.

Rosie also cross-referenced to existing evidence for PC (e), but focused on the verbal discussions she had had with various team members which confirmed and disconfirmed the information she had regarding their workloads.

Ideas for evidence

■ Use existing evidence from this and previous units.

■ Focus on a separate event and detail the information needed.

■ Personal statement.

■ Witness testimony.

■ Planning documentation.

■ Examples of information gathered.

Your ideas for evidence

Description of evidence	Location of evidence	Opportunities for cross-referencing	Reflection and analysis

K&U links

Suggested reading for knowledge and understanding purposes:

Cole, G.A., *Management: Theory and Practice,* 5th edition, chapter 27.

Mullins, L.J., *Management and Organisational Behaviour,* 4th edition, chapter 13, pp. 458–65.

Needham, D. et al., *Business for Higher Awards,* chapters 10, 11, 25, 26, 27 and 28.

Cross-referencing

Evidence and knowledge from this element can be used in the following mandatory units of NVQ Management Level 4: **A2, A4, C5, D4, B2, B3**; and the following optional units: **C10, C13, C15, G1.**

Manage your own time and resources to meet your objectives

Performance Criterion

(g) *When you need further information to take decisions, you take prompt and effective measures to obtain it.*

> This PC requires you to explain the circumstances under which additional information is needed, so you will need to give your evidence a context. This could be done by the use of a personal statement. Focus on the identified need for additional information and what it concerned. Detail the methods used to obtain it.

Interpretation

▪ Under what circumstances has the information available been insufficient to take decisions?

▪ Why was the original information insufficient?

▪ How was the need for further information identified?

▪ Who else was involved in obtaining further information?

▪ How did you go about obtaining it?

Candidate illustration

Callum drew on an instance where he had to calculate the production schedules and programmes on a predetermined part of the production process of a drilling product. He duly gathered information concerning the nature of the process, the need for materials, worker hours and productivity. Having calculated the schedules based on current customer orders and forecasted sales, Callum realised he had little information on productivity and profitability targets over the time allocated. He set about obtaining the additional information by arranging meetings with the key personnel involved in setting these targets. Evidence included the memo sent to the production manager, manufacturing manager, the finance department and sales director. The minutes of the meeting were referenced as they contained details of the additional information required.

Val focused on a project assigned to her by the head of service in her department. The project brief was to report on the implications of establishing a policy document for the introduction of flexible working hours – flexi-time – for all staff. Val initially monitored staff working hours and time keeping within the organisation to assess whether flexi-time was viable. Questionnaires were designed to evaluate staff's feelings about flexi-time and consultation was carried out across the department. Val found that while she had much useful information, she was not confident that it was representative of the whole department, since many people had not replied to her questionnaires or taken part in any of the consultation events. To ensure that the information was more reliable, Val corresponded with other similar departments and organisations to obtain information on their experiences and how other workplaces operated. This allowed her to make decisions based on national as well as local information.

Ideas for evidence

- Link to previous evidence.
- Personal statement putting circumstances into context.
- Details of correspondence requesting information from the appropriate people.
- Examples of the information obtained.

Your ideas for evidence

Description of evidence	Location of evidence	Opportunities for cross-referencing	Reflection and analysis

K&U links

Suggested reading for knowledge and understanding purposes:

Cole, G.A., *Management: Theory and Practice,* 5th edition, chapter 27.

Mullins, L.J., *Management and Organisational Behaviour,* 4th edition, chapter 13, pp. 458–65.

Needham, D. et al., *Business for Higher Awards,* chapters 10, 11, 25, 26, 27 and 28.

Cross-referencing

Evidence and knowledge from this element can be used in the following mandatory units of NVQ Management Level 4: **A2, A4, C5, D4, B2, B3**; and the following optional units: **C10, C13, C15, G1.**

Element C2.2 Manage your own time and resources to meet your objectives

Performance Criterion

(h) *You minimise unhelpful interruptions to, and digressions from, planned work.*

To meet the requirements of this PC you will need to focus on two aspects of planned work programmes: identified and unidentified interruptions and digressions. Detail the occurrences and how you have dealt with them. It is important to put the evidence into context, so you may wish to link to previous scenarios you have illustrated or write additional personal statements.

Interpretation

▌ In what circumstances have identified and unidentified digressions from planned work occurred?

▌ What were the implications and result of the digressions?

▌ How did you take action to avoid or rectify them?

Candidate illustration

Event route
To meet part of this PC's requirements, Kieron had identified likely digressions due to planned changes in EU legislation on export licences. He used his contacts at Business Link to establish tactics that would allow the company to continue trading overseas without delay in the event of the changes being implemented. Evidence concerned Kieron's communications with Business Link and the planned changes to the export licence application guidelines.

Event route
Again, meeting part of the PC's requirements, having allocated responsibility to members of her team, as detailed throughout this element, Rosie experienced a setback when one of her volunteers had to withdraw because of health problems. This was an example of an unidentified digression from planned work. The volunteer had been allocated a work programme designed to perpetuate the organisation's funding through funding applications and fundraising events. Without continuous funding, all of the planned activities would have to be reduced or some cancelled. Between recruiting a replacement, Rosie had to allocate parts of the role to existing volunteers. She did this through prioritising tasks over a three-month period and allocating work accordingly, allowing enough time to recruit a suitably qualified replacement volunteer.

Ideas for evidence

▌ Use existing evidence where appropriate.

▌ Correspondence with people concerned.

▌ Examples of changes to workplaces and practices.

▌ Personal statement justifying actions taken.

▌ Witness testimony from those concerned.

Your ideas for evidence

Description of evidence	Location of evidence	Opportunities for cross-referencing	Reflection and analysis

K&U links

Suggested reading for knowledge and understanding purposes:

Cole, G.A., *Management: Theory and Practice*, 5th edition, chapter 27.

Mullins, L.J., *Management and Organisational Behaviour*, 4th edition, chapter 13, pp. 458–65.

Needham, D. et al., *Business for Higher Awards*, chapters 10, 11, 25, 26, 27 and 28.

Cross-referencing

Evidence and knowledge from this element can be used in the following mandatory units of NVQ Management Level 4: **A2**, **A4**, **C5**, **D4**, **B2**, **B3**; and the following optional units: **C10**, **C13**, **C15**, **G1**.

| **Element** C2.2 | **Manage your own time and resources to meet your objectives** |

Performance Criterion

(i)   *You regularly review progress and reschedule activities to help achieve your planned activities.*

> This PC focuses on your review process. You should detail how and when it occurs. Explain how any changes that have been made are designed to assist in achieving objectives as planned.

Interpretation

▌ How do you review your progress and that of your team?

▌ How is review used to reschedule activities, where appropriate?

Candidate illustration

Rosie found that all the evidence could be cross-referenced from PC (h). In addition, she referenced memos from an emergency meeting called to review the reallocation and prioritisation of work. A personal statement was included which detailed the work allocation plan established as a result of the meeting.

Callum decided to focus on his experiences in developing the production schedule, as detailed in PC (g). He had pre-planned review dates, times and methods with all personnel involved and used a chart to represent these. The actual review process was illustrated with the notes from a review session with one of the production line managers.

Ideas for evidence

▌ Use existing evidence where appropriate.

▌ Personal statement explaining circumstances.

▌ Extracts from review notes or documentation.

▌ Examples of rescheduled activities.

Your ideas for evidence

Description of evidence	Location of evidence	Opportunities for cross-referencing	Reflection and analysis

K&U links

Suggested reading for knowledge and understanding purposes:

Cole, G.A., *Management: Theory and Practice*, 5th edition, chapter 27.

Mullins, L.J., *Management and Organisational Behaviour*, 4th edition, chapter 13, pp. 458–65.

Needham, D. et al., *Business for Higher Awards*, chapters 10, 11, 25, 26, 27 and 28.

Cross-referencing

Evidence and knowledge from this element can be used in the following mandatory units of NVQ Management Level 4: **A2**, **A4**, **C5**, **D4**, **B2**, **B3**; and the following optional units: **C10**, **C13**, **C15**, **G1**.

CHAPTER 7

Unit C5 Develop productive working relationships

Element C5.3 Minimise interpersonal conflict

Element C5.1 Develop the trust and support of colleagues and team members

Performance Criterion

(a) *You consult with colleagues and team members about proposed activities at appropriate times and in a manner which encourages open, frank discussion.*

> Your analysis and evidence will need to cover all aspects of this PC and the others in this element, all of which are complex in their requirements. In this case, illustrate instances where you have sought input or feedback from peers, senior colleagues and staff. Detail where these discussions or correspondence took place and explain the manner in which you requested the input.

Interpretation

- When and how do you consult colleagues?
- Do you plan for this in advance?
- When are the appropriate times for consultations?
- Do you approach different people in different ways?
- What determines your approach?

Candidate illustration

As a newly appointed manager, Callum had to build working relationships with all staff from scratch. He detailed an instance where his role required him to review shift workers' timetables to accommodate an increase in orders for drilling machinery from a major customer. In reviewing the shift patterns, Callum initially consulted with senior managers to assess the increase in production hours needed. He did this by entering an item for discussion on the agenda of the forthcoming management team meeting. The agenda and minutes were used as evidence.

Val was able to cross-reference to Unit C2, where she focused on the development of a policy and procedure report for the implementation of a flexi-time system for all staff. The evidence was highlighted to illustrate the consultation process and Val obtained a witness testimony from a senior colleague to confirm that it did encourage open and frank discussion.

Ideas for evidence

- Include evidence from previous units where appropriate.
- Video or audiotaped consultation meetings.
- Formal agendas and minutes of meetings where consultation has occurred.
- Witness testimony from people involved in consultation.
- Informal notes of input and feedback.
- Personal statement explaining circumstances, appropriateness of approach and timing.

Your ideas for evidence

Description of evidence	Location of evidence	Opportunities for cross-referencing	Reflection and analysis

K&U links Suggested reading for knowledge and understanding purposes:

Cole, G.A., *Management: Theory and Practice,* 5th edition, chapters 6, 7, 8 and 27.

Mullins, L.J., *Management and Organisational Behaviour,* 4th edition, chapters 5, 6, 7 and 8.

Needham, D. et al., *Business for Higher Awards,* chapters 10, 11 and 14.

Cross-referencing Evidence and knowledge from this element can be used in the following mandatory units of NVQ Management Level 4: **A2, A4, C2, D4, B2**; and the following optional units: **C10, C13, D2, E6, E8, F2, F4, F6, F7, G2**.

Develop the trust and support of colleagues and team members

Performance Criterion

(b) *You keep colleagues and team members informed about organisational plans and activities, emerging threats and opportunities.*

> To meet the requirements of this PC you should focus on specific plans, activities, emerging threats and opportunities. Detail their significance and explain how you communicated them; to whom was the information given, and why were they the most appropriate people? Explain your actions in dealing with the implications of the information.

Interpretation

▌ How do you keep people informed of organisational issues?

▌ How are emerging threats and opportunities identified and communicated?

▌ Do you communicate this kind of information in a way that fosters trust and support?

Candidate illustration

Kieron had begun a market analysis for potential UK sales and had expanded it to encompass Europe. Analyses of strengths, weaknesses, opportunities and threats (SWOT) had been carried out throughout the project, which meant that Kieron was able to identify threats in the form of competitors and alternative suppliers of PC software, and opportunities in the form of new market entry strategies and even potential new markets for existing products. The project was supervised by a small panel, to whom Kieron regularly presented his findings. Reports and overhead transparencies from the presentations were used as evidence.

Part of Rosie's role was to monitor trends in donations and contributions made to her organisation. She was particularly interested in identifying any seasonal trends over the previous five years and developing alternative methods of attracting donations. A recent and alarming downward trend in total donations was immediately identified, which was attributed to the introduction of a national lottery scheme. To counteract this trend, Rosie developed a strategic plan based on alternative forms of attracting funds. This plan was distributed nationally throughout the organisation as a briefing document requesting feedback from all staff. The document, together with email correspondence, was used as evidence. In addition, Rosie included a personal statement explaining her research and the process of informing staff of its implications on a local and national level.

Ideas for evidence

- Details of practices.
- Notes of formal and informal meetings.
- Reports.
- Analysis documents.
- Briefing papers.
- Personal statement explaining processes.
- Witness testimony from those involved.

Your ideas for evidence

Description of evidence	Location of evidence	Opportunities for cross-referencing	Reflection and analysis

K&U links

Suggested reading for knowledge and understanding purposes:

Cole, G.A., *Management: Theory and Practice,* 5th edition, chapters 6, 7, 8 and 27.

Mullins, L.J., *Management and Organisational Behaviour,* 4th edition, chapters 5, 6, 7 and 8.

Needham, D. et al., *Business for Higher Awards,* chapters 10, 11 and 14.

Cross-referencing

Evidence and knowledge from this element can be used in the following mandatory units of NVQ Management Level 4: **A2, A4, C2, D4, B2**; and the following optional units: **C10, C13, D2, E6, E8, F2, F4, F6, F7, G2**.

Element **C5.1** Develop the trust and support of colleagues and team members

Performance Criterion

(c) You honour the commitments you make to colleagues and team members.

> This PC will require you to focus on specific examples to illustrate your actions. Clearly, this is a key aspect in developing trust and support, so you will need to explain the implications of the commitments made and the circumstances under which they were honoured. To ensure that you meet all of the requirements of this PC, you will need to provide evidence relating to colleagues and members of your team.

Interpretation

■ What is the nature of the commitments made?

■ How do you ensure that commitments are honoured?

■ What are the consequences of failing to honour commitments?

Candidate illustration

Callum was able to continue using his review of timetables as evidence (see PC (a)). The personal implications of a change in work patterns was a major concern for the shift workers involved, since many had families to consider. Callum agreed to keep them regularly informed of the work he was doing and sought to consult with them throughout. These actions were evidenced through inclusion of the initial written request from the staff and Callum's response: a memo to all concerned setting out his plans, the reasons for change and the process of review. The memo included Callum's undertaking to consult at each stage of the review and to feed information from those affected into the decision-making process. A witness testimony from two of the staff concerned was also included.

Rosie was asked by a senior colleague to monitor the volunteers' approach to customer service, as there had been several recent complaints. This was to be done in a routine, non-threatening manner to ensure that it was fair and objective. Rosie arranged opportunities to observe customer contacts into her work schedule and was able to give weekly feedback. The request was verbal, so Rosie obtained a testimony from the senior colleague involved. Her feedback was presented in note form and was used as evidence. Rosie chose to delete the names of the staff involved to maintain confidentiality, and this was explained in a note to her assessor.

Ideas for evidence

■ Diary extracts.

■ Formal and informal correspondence with those involved.

■ Supervision documents (yours and those of your staff).

■ Witness testimony.

Your ideas for evidence

Description of evidence	Location of evidence	Opportunities for cross-referencing	Reflection and analysis

K&U links

Suggested reading for knowledge and understanding purposes:

Cole, G.A., *Management: Theory and Practice*, 5th edition, chapters 6, 7, 8 and 27.

Mullins, L.J., *Management and Organisational Behaviour*, 4th edition, chapters 5, 6, 7 and 8.

Needham, D. et al., *Business for Higher Awards*, chapters 10, 11 and 14.

Cross-referencing

Evidence and knowledge from this element can be used in the following mandatory units of NVQ Management Level 4: **A2**, **A4**, **C2**, **D4**, **B2**; and the following optional units: **C10**, **C13**, **D2**, **E6**, **E8**, **F2**, **F4**, **F6**, **F7**, **G2**.

Element C5.1   Develop the trust and support of colleagues and team members

Performance Criterion

(d) You treat colleagues and team members in a manner which shows your respect for individuals and the need for confidentiality.

> As with PC (c), you will need to focus on specific instances in order to meet the requirements of this performance criterion. Identify occurrences where you have had to show respect and maintain confidentiality in order to develop trust and support. The examples need not be extreme, but they should show your ability to empathise with the issues concerned. Illustrate your evidence by explaining the circumstances and the outcome of your involvement.

Interpretation

- What is your personal approach to interpersonal communication?
- What skills do you employ in developing trust and support?
- Do you treat all colleagues and team members in the same way?
- How do you maintain confidentiality when necessary?

Candidate illustration

Val focused on a team meeting in which she questioned an individual member of staff about his unacceptable conduct in the office. This was done publicly to ensure that the individual realised the effect of his behaviour on the rest of the team. However, during the meeting, it became clear to Val that the behaviour was a consequence of personal problems, so she immediately ended the conversation, moved on to other issues, and arranged to meet the member of staff later to avoid further discomfort and to seek ways to address the issue. Val met the staff member in a private office, away from the workplace, to ensure that confidentiality was maintained. Val included the minutes from the meeting when the problem was initially discussed and a testimony from the member of staff involved.

Kieron was experiencing difficulties with two members of his team, who seemed unwilling to contribute ideas during team meetings and development sessions. He felt able to manage the situation, but sought advice from a senior colleague as to the best way to take action. Kieron arranged to meet his colleague during the lunch hour to discuss the issue informally. He sought advice on the problems he was experiencing, but did not name the individuals concerned. As a result of the advice he had been given, Kieron approached each of the two members of staff using slightly different methods, which proved more successful.

Ideas for evidence

- Personal statement detailing circumstances and actions taken.
- Witness testimony from those concerned.
- Notes of meetings.
- Supervision documents.
- Formal communications.

Your ideas for evidence

Description of evidence	Location of evidence	Opportunities for cross-referencing	Reflection and analysis

K&U links

Suggested reading for knowledge and understanding purposes:

Cole, G.A., *Management: Theory and Practice*, 5th edition, chapters 6, 7, 8 and 27.

Mullins, L.J., *Management and Organisational Behaviour*, 4th edition, chapters 5, 6, 7 and 8.

Needham, D. et al., *Business for Higher Awards*, chapters 10, 11 and 14.

Cross-referencing

Evidence and knowledge from this element can be used in the following mandatory units of NVQ Management Level 4: **A2**, **A4**, **C2**, **D4**, **B2**; and the following optional units: **C10**, **C13**, **D2**, **E6**, **E8**, **F2**, **F4**, **F6**, **F7**, **G2**.

Element C5.1   Develop the trust and support of colleagues and team members

Performance Criterion

(e) *You give colleagues and team members sufficient support for them to achieve their work objectives.*

> For this PC, evidence can relate to support that has been requested or volunteered. Detail the kinds of support given and explain how it was designed to assist in achieving work objectives. Explain your approach and why the support was appropriate.

Interpretation

▪ What type of support do you give?

▪ How do you ensure that support is appropriate and sufficient?

▪ How do you ensure that the support you give is practical?

Candidate illustration

Callum was able to utilise evidence already included in this element. He highlighted examples where he had given support to shift workers to enable them to maintain outputs despite changes in working hours. The support took the form of a week-long handover period, in which workers were able to become accustomed gradually to changes in times, work routines and different equipment.

Val cross-referenced to her evidence concerning the disruptive office worker (PC (d)). Because of his personal circumstances, he needed the opportunity to work from home one day a week. Val sought authority to agree to this and arranged for the employee to have a pager on these days so that he could be easily contacted. The request for authority was submitted as evidence, together with a testimony from the staff member concerned and an extract from an equipment book showing the supply of the pager. The circumstances were clearly explained in Val's analysis.

Ideas for evidence

▪ Supervision documents.

▪ Memos.

▪ Correspondence.

▪ Extracts from reports.

▪ Details of support given; time; equipment; advice.

▪ Witness testimony from staff and colleagues involved.

Your ideas for evidence

Description of evidence	Location of evidence	Opportunities for cross-referencing	Reflection and analysis

K&U links

Suggested reading for knowledge and understanding purposes:

Cole, G.A., *Management: Theory and Practice*, 5th edition, chapters 6, 7, 8 and 27.

Mullins, L.J., *Management and Organisational Behaviour*, 4th edition, chapters 5, 6, 7 and 8.

Needham, D. et al., *Business for Higher Awards*, chapters 10, 11 and 14.

Cross-referencing

Evidence and knowledge from this element can be used in the following mandatory units of NVQ Management Level 4: **A2**, **A4**, **C2**, **D4**, **B2**; and the following optional units: **C10**, **C13**, **D2**, **E6**, **E8**, **F2**, **F4**, **F6**, **F7**, **G2**.

Element C5.1 Develop the trust and support of colleagues and team members

Performance Criterion

(f) You discuss discreetly with the colleagues and team members concerned your evaluation of their work and behaviour.

If you have a formal process of supervision and appraisal within your organisation, explain how it is used to monitor and evaluate work and behaviour. If not, detail instances where you have provided feedback and sought a response from staff regarding their work. This need not be due to extremes of performance.

Interpretation

- How are matters relating to work and behaviour dealt with?
- How are issues raised and discussed?
- How do you undertake evaluations of work?

Candidate illustration

Rosie utilised supervision and appraisal records from two members of staff. In her organisation, all supervision is one to one, and therefore it met the requirement of being discreet. The records themselves detailed timescales and targets, work allocations and expected standards of practice. Each team member discussed these areas in supervision and was appraised using quantitative and qualitative methods. Rosie highlighted that the outcomes of appraisal were used as a basis for staff training and development and as a means of highlighting good practices.

Working for a small organisation, Kieron did not use formal processes to feedback evaluations to staff. However, he did monitor the achievement of sales targets for each staff member and discuss letters and messages from customers, both positive and negative, with the sales people concerned on a one-to-one basis, if necessary. Monitoring occurred regularly and Kieron submitted evidence consisting of monitoring charts and letters from customers, together with notes of the evaluations given to staff. The evidence was confirmed through testimony from one of the sales people involved and from a senior manager in the company.

Ideas for evidence

- Supervision and appraisal documentation.
- Monitoring information.
- Details of basis of evaluations.
- Letters from customers.
- Achievement or underachievement of targets and objectives.
- Witness testimony from those involved.
- Notes of discussions held with staff and colleagues.

Your ideas for evidence

Description of evidence	Location of evidence	Opportunities for cross-referencing	Reflection and analysis

K&U links

Suggested reading for knowledge and understanding purposes:

Cole, G.A., *Management: Theory and Practice,* 5th edition, chapters 6, 7, 8 and 27.

Mullins, L.J., *Management and Organisational Behaviour,* 4th edition, chapters 5, 6, 7 and 8.

Needham, D. et al., *Business for Higher Awards,* chapters 10, 11 and 14.

Cross-referencing

Evidence and knowledge from this element can be used in the following mandatory units of NVQ Management Level 4: **A2**, **A4**, **C2**, **D4**, **B2**; and the following optional units: **C10**, **C13**, **D2**, **E6**, **E8**, **F2**, **F4**, **F6**, **F7**, **G2**.

Element C5.2 | Develop the trust and support of your manager

Performance Criterion

(a) *You give your manager timely and accurate reports on activities, results and achievements.*

> You will need to explain evidence relating to the above range of areas. Detail why particular times are appropriate and the level of accuracy required. Keeping your manager informed could be part of a regular, structured process, or it may happen informally as and when appropriate. Explain your approach to developing the trust and support of your manager through communication and reporting.

Interpretation

▌ How do you keep your manager informed?

▌ What is the appropriate level of detail?

▌ When does this occur?

Candidate illustration

Val's organisation has structured supervision and appraisal procedures for all staff and their managers. The main focus is on work-related issues. Val was able to include supervision documentation that clearly met the range of areas detailed in the performance criteria. She decided to include a number of instances relating to various aspects of her job to show consistency over a period of time. She also obtained a witness testimony from her line manager, which covered all aspects of this element. She annotated the testimony in order to link it clearly to each performance criterion.

Kieron did not have a formal method of reporting to his line manager, who was the owner of the company. As a matter of professional practice, he did include analysis of sales figures whenever reports were requested. Kieron occasionally gave presentations to his manager and other senior staff on current activities and projected sales. These presentations always ended with question and answer sessions that allowed Kieron and the managers to explore ideas and investigate previous achievements. Kieron included a written report as evidence and a cassette tape of one of his presentations that took place as he was progressing this unit. The content of the tape was fully explained in his analysis.

Ideas for evidence

▌ Supervision and appraisal documentation.

▌ Notes of informal meetings.

▌ Progress reports detailing results, outcomes and plans.

▌ Witness testimony from your manager.

▌ Video or audio tape of briefing sessions with your manager.

Your ideas for evidence

Description of evidence	Location of evidence	Opportunities for cross-referencing	Reflection and analysis

K&U links

Suggested reading for knowledge and understanding purposes:

Cole, G.A., *Management: Theory and Practice,* 5th edition, chapters 6, 7, 26 and 27.

Mullins, L.J., *Management and Organisational Behaviour,* 4th edition, chapters 4, 5, 8, 10 and 13.

Needham, D. et al., *Business for Higher Awards,* chapters 10, 11 and 14.

Cross-referencing

Evidence and knowledge from this element can be used in the following mandatory units of NVQ Management Level 4: **A2**, **A4**, **C2**, **D4**, **B2**, **B3**; and the following optional units: **C13**, **C15**, **F7**.

Element C5.2 Develop the trust and support of your manager

Performance Criterion

(b) *You give your manager clear and accurate information about emerging threats and opportunities with a degree of urgency appropriate to the situation.*

> To complete this PC you will need to focus on specific incidents and explain your role, and the role of your manager, in exchanges of data and information relating to emerging threats and opportunities. Explain why timescales are appropriate and detail how these actions contribute to developing the trust and support of your manager.

Interpretation

- What kind of information do you provide to your manager?
- How are emerging threats and opportunities identified and communicated?
- What is the likely nature of these threats and opportunities?
- What timescales are appropriate? Is this detailed by the nature of the information?

Candidate illustration

Kieron was able to cross-reference to evidence detailing a report he had prepared for his manager on market entry strategies in European countries (see Element C5.1, PC (b)).

Val drew on her records of supervision she had with her line manager. The structured approach to supervision and the noting of discussions allowed her to highlight information passed to her manager and the discussions that took place, including action points for each one, depending on the urgency of the situation.

Ideas for evidence

- Cross-reference to previous evidence, if appropriate.
- Memos sent to your manager, and replies.
- Reports presented by you.
- Notes of discussions.
- Materials from presentations given by you.
- Notes of supervision.
- Personal statement detailing level of urgency and timescales.

Your ideas for evidence

Description of evidence	Location of evidence	Opportunities for cross-referencing	Reflection and analysis

K&U links   Suggested reading for knowledge and understanding purposes:

Cole, G.A., *Management: Theory and Practice,* 5th edition, chapters 6, 7, 26 and 27.

Mullins, L.J., *Management and Organisational Behaviour,* 4th edition, chapters 4, 5, 8, 10 and 13.

Needham, D. et al., *Business for Higher Awards,* chapters 10, 11 and 14.

Cross-referencing   Evidence and knowledge from this element can be used in the following mandatory units of NVQ Management Level 4: **A2, A4, C2, D4, B2, B3**; and the following optional units: **C13, C15, F7**.

Element C5.2 | Develop the trust and support of your manager

Performance Criterion

(c) You consult your manager about organisational policies and ways of working at appropriate times.

Examine the circumstances that determine your need to consult regarding policy and policy implementation, and the identification of appropriate ways of working. Detail your approach to the situation. Your evidence does not have to cover a whole policy, but could simply relate to the fine-tuning of an approach to work. Focus on what you were trying to achieve and how your manager assisted you.

Interpretation

How is advice sought?

In what circumstances have you consulted?

How do you gauge appropriate times?

Candidate illustration

Callum became involved in staff recruitment and selection almost as soon as he joined the company. Although conversant with the organisation's guidelines regarding the process, he was unclear as to how to action them. During a progress review session, Callum asked his line manager to explain what was required of him as a member of an interview panel. His manager explained that standard documentation was used to aid objectivity. Callum obtained the documentation from the personnel department in preparation, and even carried out a practice run with a colleague (who played the role of interviewee) to familiarise himself with it! As evidence, he submitted the practice run documentation, a witness testimony from his manager explaining the circumstances, and the documentation used in the actual interview process. Callum deleted the names of the prospective candidates to maintain confidentiality.

Rosie detailed information and guidance obtained from her manager regarding staff replacement due to sickness and absenteeism. This was discussed during a progress review as Rosie had to reallocate work in order to maintain the progress of her team. Notes of the meeting were submitted as evidence, together with a personal statement from Rosie explaining the situation.

Ideas for evidence

Evidence of discussions with and information obtained from your manager.

Supervision documentation.

Witness testimony from your manager.

Personal statement detailing circumstances.

Your ideas for evidence

Description of evidence	Location of evidence	Opportunities for cross-referencing	Reflection and analysis

K&U links

Suggested reading for knowledge and understanding purposes:

Cole, G.A., *Management: Theory and Practice,* 5th edition, chapters 6, 7, 26 and 27.

Mullins, L.J., *Management and Organisational Behaviour,* 4th edition, chapters 4, 5, 8, 10 and 13.

Needham, D. et al., *Business for Higher Awards,* chapters 10, 11 and 14.

Cross-referencing

Evidence and knowledge from this element can be used in the following mandatory units of NVQ Management Level 4: **A2, A4, C2, D4, B2, B3**; and the following optional units: **C13, C15, F7**.

Develop the trust and support of your manager

Performance Criterion

(d) Your proposals for action are clear and realistic.

> Please read PC (e) before identifying evidence as this may well reduce the amount of work you need to do. You will probably already have this kind of evidence in your portfolio, so make use of it. Your analysis should demonstrate your ability to formulate clear and realistic proposals. Focus on specific examples in your evidence and explain how you ensured that proposals were clear and achievable. To ensure that you meet all the evidence requirements, proposals must be both written and spoken. Spoken proposals could take the form of a discussion or a presentation.

Interpretation

- Cross-reference to existing evidence, if appropriate.
- When have you proposed action?
- How has it been proposed?
- What measures do you take to ensure that proposals are clear and realistic?

Candidate illustration

Kieron again cross-referenced to the reports that he presented to the project panel on market entry strategies (see Element C5.1, PC (b), and PC (b) of this element). For this evidence, Kieron highlighted the facts and figures section of his report, which contained European legal requirements and the projected cost of compliance. In addition, he referenced the sources of his information and the calculations he had undertaken in conjunction with the company accountant. A witness testimony from the accountant was also included.

Rosie focused on a report she had submitted proposing revisions to her team's structure. The proposal was based on an identified need to delegate responsibility and develop managers for the future. The proposal contained costings for the appointment of a team leader who would be managed by Rosie. Costs were met from Rosie's existing budget and rationalised through cost–benefit analysis.

Ideas for evidence

- Link to PC (e) of this element.
- Cross-reference to existing evidence, if appropriate.
- Evidence of written *and* spoken proposals.
- Calculations and analysis that ensure accuracy.
- Other sources of information.
- Witness testimony from others involved.

Your ideas for evidence

Description of evidence	Location of evidence	Opportunities for cross-referencing	Reflection and analysis

K&U links

Suggested reading for knowledge and understanding purposes:

Cole, G.A., *Management: Theory and Practice,* 5th edition, chapters 6, 7, 26 and 27.

Mullins, L.J., *Management and Organisational Behaviour,* 4th edition, chapters 4, 5, 8, 10 and 13.

Needham, D. et al., *Business for Higher Awards,* chapters 10, 11 and 14.

Cross-referencing

Evidence and knowledge from this element can be used in the following mandatory units of NVQ Management Level 4: **A2, A4, C2, D4, B2, B3**; and the following optional units: **C13, C15, F7**.

Element **C5.2**	# Develop the trust and support of your manager

Performance Criterion

(e) *You present your proposals for action to your manager at appropriate times.*

> Clearly, this PC can be linked to the evidence for PCs (a) to (d) to avoid repetition. Focus on and explain why timing is so appropriate.

Interpretation

- How did you ensure that proposals are presented at an appropriate time?
- Are there any determined times set aside for this kind of activity?
- Do opportunities need to be made?
- Do some circumstances dictate urgency?

Candidate illustration

Both Kieron and Rosie cross-referenced to PC (d). They needed personal statements and witness testimonies from their managers detailing the appropriateness of timing and the circumstances surrounding the proposals.

Your ideas for evidence

Description of evidence	Location of evidence	Opportunities for cross-referencing	Reflection and analysis

K&U links

Suggested reading for knowledge and understanding purposes:

Cole, G.A., *Management: Theory and Practice*, 5th edition, chapters 6, 7, 26 and 27.

Mullins, L.J., *Management and Organisational Behaviour*, 4th edition, chapters 4, 5, 8, 10 and 13.

Needham, D. et al., *Business for Higher Awards*, chapters 10, 11 and 14.

Cross-referencing

Evidence and knowledge from this element can be used in the following mandatory units of NVQ Management Level 4: **A2**, **A4**, **C2**, **D4**, **B2**, **B3**; and the following optional units: **C13**, **C15**, **F7**.

Element C5.2 Develop the trust and support of your manager

Performance Criterion

(f) *Where you have disagreements with your manager, you make constructive efforts to resolve these disagreements and maintain a good working relationship.*

> This PC will require you to identify specific instances where you have had to take action as a result of a disagreement with your manager. Explain the situation and detail how you conducted yourself to ensure that trust and support were maintained.

Interpretation

▌ In what circumstances have you had disagreements with your manager?

▌ How have you made efforts to rectify the situation?

▌ What have the outcomes been?

▌ Was a mutually agreeable course of action identified?

▌ What did you learn from the experience?

Candidate illustration

Callum was dissatisfied with the managerial responsibility allocated to him in his first six months. It seemed he had been given rather menial tasks to do rather than ones that would give him any management experience, and he tackled his manager about this during supervision. His manager did not share Callum's concern, pointing out that as a trainee manager Callum needed experience on which to base his management of staff. Callum continued to feel dissatisfied. His manager then explained that Callum would be allocated staff to manage after one year. Callum took the initiative to request the opportunity to shadow his manager, to which his manager agreed, subject to the employees concerned giving their consent. In this way, Callum felt that he would get some additional management experience without compromising his relationship with his manager.

In Val's organisation, the lines of authority were clearly identified to ensure accountability. One week, Val had responded to an important request from her branch director without informing or briefing her manager on his return to the office. Val's manager was subsequently placed in an embarrassing position during a meeting with the branch director when he appeared ignorant of the request. He was angry that Val had failed to inform him and requested that she keep him fully informed in future. Val endeavoured to do this, using internal email as a means of communication. She also began to note issues that would be relevant to her manager. A witness testimony from her manager was further proof that this matter had been resolved.

Ideas for evidence

- Memos to or from your manager.
- Personal statement detailing the situation and how it was handled.
- Witness testimony from your line manager.
- Notes of meetings – outcomes of agreed action.

Your ideas for evidence

Description of evidence	Location of evidence	Opportunities for cross-referencing	Reflection and analysis

K&U links

Suggested reading for knowledge and understanding purposes:

Cole, G.A., *Management: Theory and Practice,* 5th edition, chapters 6, 7, 26 and 27.

Mullins, L.J., *Management and Organisational Behaviour,* 4th edition, chapters 4, 5, 8, 10 and 13.

Needham, D. et al., *Business for Higher Awards,* chapters 10, 11 and 14.

Cross-referencing

Evidence and knowledge from this element can be used in the following mandatory units of NVQ Management Level 4: **A2**, **A4**, **C2**, **D4**, **B2**, **B3**; and the following optional units: **C13**, **C15**, **F7**.

Element C5.3 Minimise interpersonal conflict

Performance Criterion

(a) *You inform individuals of the standards of work and behaviour you expect in a manner, and at a level and pace appropriate to the individuals involved.*

> You will need to detail and evidence your skills in communicating information about expected standards of work and behaviour in a way that is meaningful to the recipient. Focus on specific situations and explain your approach.

Interpretation

- Focus on team members, colleagues or senior colleagues.
- How are expected standards of work and behaviour identified?
- How is the appropriate manner, level and pace of communication gauged?

Candidate illustration

Event route

A routine part of Kieron's role was the continuous monitoring of the customer service provided by his sales team and the support personnel involved in after-sales service. He did this by occasionally accompanying staff on their visits to customers' premises. The guidelines issued to staff at the customer interface were used to evaluate the level of service provided. Kieron explained this process in his analysis and evidenced the written feedback given to two members of staff, one feedback sheet confirming good practices and the other requiring improved standards of service. He also included notes of conversations held with staff about the feedback sheets.

Event route

Rosie was able to cross-reference to Element C5.1, PC (d), where she had had to explain standards of work and behaviour expected in the office. Notes of the conversations, together with a witness testimony from the member of staff concerned, were submitted as evidence.

Ideas for evidence

- Notes of conversations with individuals.
- Personal statement detailing circumstances.
- Witness testimony from individuals concerned.
- Written feedback or instruction provided to individuals.

Your ideas for evidence

Description of evidence	Location of evidence	Opportunities for cross-referencing	Reflection and analysis

K&U links

Suggested reading for knowledge and understanding purposes:

Cole, G.A., *Management: Theory and Practice,* 5th edition, chapter 26.

Mullins, L.J., *Management and Organisational Behaviour,* 4th edition, chapters 4, 5, 6, 7 and 20, pp. 722–8.

Needham, D. et al., *Business for Higher Awards,* chapters 10, 11 and 14.

Cross-referencing

Evidence and knowledge from this element can be used in the following mandatory units of NVQ Management Level 4: **A2**, **A4**; and the following optional units: **C10**, **C13**, **C15**, **F2**, **F4**, **F6**, **F7**.

Element C5.3 **Minimise interpersonal conflict**

Performance Criterion

(b) *You provide opportunities for individuals to discuss problems which directly or indirectly affect their work.*

Explain the steps that you take to ensure that these opportunities are available. Detail your approach to interpersonal issues. Your evidence should cover instances where staff have discussed work-related or personal problems.

Interpretation

- How are opportunities provided?
- Are these formal or informal?
- Are opportunities routine or non-routine?
- In what way does discussion of these types of issues reduce the likelihood of interpersonal conflict?

Candidate illustration

Although leading a team of staff, Callum did not have direct management responsibility for them. He projected himself as open and approachable, often discussing work and personal issues with peers, colleagues and staff. Unfortunately, these instances were all informal and not noted. To highlight competence in this area, Callum prepared a short report detailing two such discussions, with the permission of the people involved. His role was to listen and suggest constructive ways to reduce conflict between team members and departments. He detailed conversations, explaining why he had made suggestions and the outcome of the incidents. He obtained two testimonies from each of the individuals concerned. Callum also looked at the rest of this element and was able to cover the majority of the performance criteria requirements in his report.

Val was able to use copies of supervision documents with members of her team. She selected two, where conflict had been avoided through initial individual discussions with the people involved, followed by a group meeting in which the two were able to find their own solutions. In a personal statement Val detailed her role as mediator and explained why it was important for those involved to take ownership of the situation and find solutions themselves.

Ideas for evidence

- Reports detailing your approach to specific situations.
- Witness testimony from those involved.
- Supervision documentation.

Your ideas for evidence

Description of evidence	Location of evidence	Opportunities for cross-referencing	Reflection and analysis

K&U links

Suggested reading for knowledge and understanding purposes:

Cole, G.A., *Management: Theory and Practice*, 5th edition, chapter 26.

Mullins, L.J., *Management and Organisational Behaviour*, 4th edition, chapters 4, 5, 6, 7 and 20, pp. 722–8.

Needham, D. et al., *Business for Higher Awards*, chapters 10, 11 and 14.

Cross-referencing

Evidence and knowledge from this element can be used in the following mandatory units of NVQ Management Level 4: **A2**, **A4**; and the following optional units: **C10**, **C13**, **C15**, **F2**, **F4**, **F6**, **F7**.

Element C5.3 Minimise interpersonal conflict

Performance Criterion

(c) You take prompt action to deal with conflicts between individuals.

Clearly, evidence and analysis for this performance criterion should be linked to PC (b) in this element. Explain the approach taken in dealing with conflicts.

Interpretation

■ Are all conflicts between individuals self-evident?

■ How do you identify conflict situations?

■ What action have you taken or suggested to those involved?

Candidate illustration

Both Val and Callum continued to use evidence drawn from the events detailed for PC (b).

Ideas for evidence

■ A personal report detailing your approach and actions taken.

■ Witness testimony from those involved.

■ Supervision documentation detailing actions to be taken by you.

■ Cross-reference to existing evidence.

Your ideas for evidence

Description of evidence	Location of evidence	Opportunities for cross-referencing	Reflection and analysis

K&U links

Suggested reading for knowledge and understanding purposes:

Cole, G.A., *Management: Theory and Practice,* 5th edition, chapter 26.

Mullins, L.J., *Management and Organisational Behaviour,* 4th edition, chapters 4, 5, 6, 7 and 20, pp. 722–8.

Needham, D. et al., *Business for Higher Awards,* chapters 10, 11 and 14.

Cross-referencing

Evidence and knowledge from this element can be used in the following mandatory units of NVQ Management Level 4: **A2**, **A4**; and the following optional units: **C10**, **C13**, **C15**, **F2**, **F4**, **F6**, **F7**.

Element C5.3 Minimise interpersonal conflict

Performance Criterion

(d) You inform relevant people about conflicts outside your area of responsibility.

Make sure you focus on specific incidents. Detail your involvement in informing others of the situation and making recommendations for conflict resolution. Relevant people could be higher-level managers, colleagues or specialists such as personnel or counsellors.

Interpretation

▌ In what circumstances have you been involved with conflicts outside your area of responsibility?

▌ Who has been the most appropriate person to contact?

▌ What information have you given them?

Candidate illustration

Kieron focused on a scenario involving conflict between two administrative staff over work allocation, which resulted in the production of sales figures being delayed. Kieron approached both of the people concerned to help resolve the problem. Finding it to be an interpersonal conflict, he discussed the problem with the office manager, who had been unaware of the situation. Kieron used the memo sent to the office manager as evidence, together with a personal statement explaining the situation and actions taken.

Val detailed a situation in which she had contacted the corporate personnel office for information on procedures regarding conflict between peers. As evidence she used the email sent to personnel, together with a witness testimony from the personnel officer involved. The testimony explained the recommendations made and how they were in keeping with the department's policy.

Ideas for evidence

▌ Cross-references to existing evidence, if appropriate.

▌ Personnel report or statement detailing the situation and actions taken.

▌ Memos and emails sent to appropriate people.

▌ Witness testimony from those involved.

Your ideas for evidence

Description of evidence	Location of evidence	Opportunities for cross-referencing	Reflection and analysis

K&U links

Suggested reading for knowledge and understanding purposes:

Cole, G.A., *Management: Theory and Practice*, 5th edition, chapter 26.

Mullins, L.J., *Management and Organisational Behaviour*, 4th edition, chapters 4, 5, 6, 7 and 20, pp. 722–8.

Needham, D. et al., *Business for Higher Awards*, chapters 10, 11 and 14.

Cross-referencing

Evidence and knowledge from this element can be used in the following mandatory units of NVQ Management Level 4: **A2**, **A4**; and the following optional units: **C10**, **C13**, **C15**, **F2**, **F4**, **F6**, **F7**.

Element C5.3 Minimise interpersonal conflict

Performance Criterion

(e) The ways you resolve conflicts minimise disruption to work and discord between individuals.

> Again, you may be able to cross-reference to existing evidence in this element. Detail the approach you have taken to avoid the negative outcomes of conflict resolution. Explain the actions taken and what was achieved.

Interpretation

▌ How have you ensured minimum disruption?

▌ What actions have you taken to reduce or avoid discord between those involved?

▌ Which skills have you used to do this?

Candidate illustration

Val was able to cross-reference once more to the scenario originally evidenced in Element C5.1, PC (d). She explained the actions taken in her analysis. She had broached the issue in a team meeting to promote discussion among the team, but, finding the matter to be of a personal nature, she discussed the problem in confidence with the individual concerned. In this way, she ensured both that the team was aware of the issue and had an opportunity to discuss it, and that the individual team member was given support in resolving the situation. The assistance given to the individual – a temporary flexibility of office hours – reduced disruption to work as the individual was able to continue working at home. Discord between the team and the individual was reduced through open discussion and the team meeting.

Kieron cross-referenced to evidence used in PC (d) of this element as it related to discord and disruption of work. In his analysis he explained why he had taken steps to inform the office manager and the result of his actions, which were to maintain the availability of sales figures for management and cost-accounting purposes, and the achievement of targets and bonus allocations.

Your ideas for evidence

Description of evidence	Location of evidence	Opportunities for cross-referencing	Reflection and analysis

K&U links

Suggested reading for knowledge and understanding purposes:

Cole, G.A., *Management: Theory and Practice,* 5th edition, chapter 26.

Mullins, L.J., *Management and Organisational Behaviour,* 4th edition, chapters 4, 5, 6, 7 and 20, pp. 722–8.

Needham, D. et al., *Business for Higher Awards,* chapters 10, 11 and 14.

Cross-referencing

Evidence and knowledge from this element can be used in the following mandatory units of NVQ Management Level 4: **A2**, **A4**; and the following optional units: **C10**, **C13**, **C15**, **F2**, **F4**, **F6**, **F7**.

Element C5.3   Minimise interpersonal conflict

**Performance
Criterion**

*(f)   The way you resolve conflict complies with organisational and
legal requirements.*

> You should evidence your role in managing conflict situations on
> behalf of your organisation. Explain how procedures or policies
> support those involved in complying with any legal requirements.

Interpretation

▌ How has your knowledge of organisational requirements and
legislation informed your actions when dealing with
interpersonal conflict?

**Candidate
illustration**

Val highlighted the use of the supervision process within her
organisation as a tool for identifying and dealing with potential and
actual conflicts. Her role, as detailed in PC (b), was to assist as a
mediator and help those concerned to explore methods of resolving
conflicts at a local level.

Callum found this performance criterion difficult to meet as he was
relatively new to the organisation. To meet requirements, he compiled
a brief report detailing the knowledge of organisational and legal
requirements he felt would impact on the formal management of
interpersonal conflict. These included the Sex Discrimination Act,
Race Relations Act, Health and Safety at Work Act, principles of
equal opportunities and valuing diversity, sickness and absenteeism
procedures, supervision and appraisal, training and development,
and disciplinary and grievance procedures. The report was supported
by a witness testimony from his line manager confirming Callum's
knowledge and his ability to apply it to conflict situations.

Ideas for evidence

▌ Cross-reference to evidence from previous elements or
performance criteria, if appropriate.

▌ Personal reports detailing knowledge and application of
organisational and legal requirements to conflict situations.

▌ Evidence relating to following procedures such as disciplinary or
guidance documentation.

▌ Supervision documents.

▌ Notes of conversations.

▌ Supporting witness testimony from those involved.

Your ideas for evidence

Description of evidence	Location of evidence	Opportunities for cross-referencing	Reflection and analysis

K&U links

Suggested reading for knowledge and understanding purposes:

Cole, G.A., *Management: Theory and Practice,* 5th edition, chapter 26.

Mullins, L.J., *Management and Organisational Behaviour,* 4th edition, chapters 4, 5, 6, 7 and 20, pp. 722–8.

Needham, D. et al., *Business for Higher Awards,* chapters 10, 11 and 14.

Cross-referencing

Evidence and knowledge from this element can be used in the following mandatory units of NVQ Management Level 4: **A2**, **A4**; and the following optional units: **C10**, **C13**, **C15**, **F2**, **F4**, **F6**, **F7**.

Element C5.3 Minimise interpersonal conflict

Performance Criterion

(g) *Your records of conflicts and their outcomes are accurate, and comply with requirements for confidentiality and other organisational policies.*

> Explain your records system and evidence samples. Detail how you ensure that confidentiality is maintained. Include any other requirements that are specific to your area of work.

Interpretation

- Why is accuracy important?
- Which records are kept?
- Why are they kept?
- In addition to issues surrounding confidentiality, what other organisational requirements impact on how records are kept?

Candidate illustration

Again, Val focused on supervision procedures and the noting of discussions and actions to be taken. She also detailed the system for storage of the documents that ensured confidentiality of discussions and actions on behalf of those staff concerned. She invited her assessor to her office to observe these records, to help maintain confidentiality.

Kieron detailed his record-keeping system and explained the role of administrative staff in storing and maintaining records. He detailed his knowledge of the requirements of his organisation and obtained a witness testimony from a senior administrative employee, which confirmed the accuracy of his recording and that he ensured records were forwarded to the correct people. Kieron also included an example of a sickness and absenteeism document completed as a result of conflict within his team.

Ideas for evidence

- Personal statement detailing how documents are stored and retrieved to ensure confidentiality.
- Examples of documents to highlight accuracy.
- Personal statement from others involved.

Your ideas for evidence

Description of evidence	Location of evidence	Opportunities for cross-referencing	Reflection and analysis

K&U links

Suggested reading for knowledge and understanding purposes:

Cole, G.A., *Management: Theory and Practice,* 5th edition, chapter 26.

Mullins, L.J., *Management and Organisational Behaviour,* 4th edition, chapters 4, 5, 6, 7 and 20, pp. 722–8.

Needham, D. et al., *Business for Higher Awards,* chapters 10, 11 and 14.

Cross-referencing

Evidence and knowledge from this element can be used in the following mandatory units of NVQ Management Level 4: **A2**, **A4**; and the following optional units: **C10**, **C13**, **C15**, **F2**, **F4**, **F6**, **F7**.

Element C5.3 **Minimise interpersonal conflict**

| **Performance Criterion** | (h) *You make recommendations for improving procedures and reducing the potential for conflict promptly to the relevant people.* |

> Focus on incidents where you have made minor or major changes to any procedures that impact on conflict resolution. These could be specific to the incidents you have had to deal with rather than relating to permanent changes.

Interpretation

- Under which circumstances have you made recommendations?
- To whom were they made?
- What did they concern?
- What were the outcomes of the changes, as recommended?

Candidate illustration

Kieron focused on the scenario he detailed for PC (d) involving conflict between two administrative staff. Informing their manager of the situation, Kieron recommended that one be given clear responsibility for the compilation and supply of sales figures. In this way, he would know who to consult regarding the figures and the difficulties between the administrative staff would be partially resolved. Kieron cross-referenced to the memo he sent and obtained a testimony from the office manager confirming that his suggestion was implemented.

Val explained how she had recommended introducing an action points column to existing supervision documents. These would increase the accountability of the parties involved and make review of progress easier. She submitted the letter that detailed and justified the changes as evidence, together with a personal statement explaining the implications.

Your ideas for evidence

Description of evidence	Location of evidence	Opportunities for cross-referencing	Reflection and analysis

K&U links

Suggested reading for knowledge and understanding purposes:

Cole, G.A., *Management: Theory and Practice*, 5th edition, chapter 26.

Mullins, L.J., *Management and Organisational Behaviour*, 4th edition, chapters 4, 5, 6, 7 and 20, pp. 722–8.

Needham, D. et al., *Business for Higher Awards*, chapters 10, 11 and 14.

Cross-referencing

Evidence and knowledge from this element can be used in the following mandatory units of NVQ Management Level 4: **A2**, **A4**; and the following optional units: **C10**, **C13**, **C15**, **F2**, **F4**, **F6**, **F7**.

CHAPTER 8

Unit D4 Provide information to support decision making

Element D4.3   Analyse information to support decision making

Element D4.4   Advise and inform others

Element D4.1   Obtain information for decision making

Performance Criterion

(a) You identify the information you need to make the required decisions.

To meet the requirements of this PC you will need to detail a specific instance where you have needed to obtain information for decision-making purposes. Explain how you identified the information needed. This need not be a major decision – a routine decision would be perfectly acceptable.

Interpretation

◼ How is information identified?

◼ How do impending decisions inform on the kinds of information needed?

Candidate illustration

Event route

Val focused on decisions based around the allocation of budget amounts to specific areas of her work, in particular staffing, travel, stationery and subcontracting. She based her decisions on information relating to the previous year's expenditure: priorities for service development and the projected spend. This was reflected in her annual budgetary report, which she was able to reference throughout the element.

Kieron's approach was to evidence factual information he had obtained to justify the decision to create a new job within his team. The information related to increases in sales and customers, and the increased travelling required of his existing sales team. In particular, expansion into the European market required the recruitment of sales agents. Kieron included the factual information and detailed why it justified the extra member of staff.

Ideas for evidence

◼ Examples of actual information that has been used to inform decisions.

◼ Explanations as to why it was needed.

◼ Reports that link information to decisions.

Your ideas for evidence

Description of evidence	Location of evidence	Opportunities for cross-referencing	Reflection and analysis

K&U links

Suggested reading for knowledge and understanding purposes:

Cole, G.A., *Management: Theory and Practice,* 5th edition, chapters 19 and 28, pp. 227–8.

Mullins, L.J., *Management and Organisational Behaviour,* 4th edition, chapter 2, pp. 57–8, chapter 9, pp. 292–305.

Needham, D. et al., *Business for Higher Awards,* chapters 9, 26, 27 and 28.

Cross-referencing

This element could be cross-referenced to any unit, depending on the nature of the evidence selected.

Element D4.1 Obtain information for decision making

Performance Criterion

(b) The sources of information which you use are reliable, and sufficiently wide-ranging to meet current and likely future information requirements.

You will need to detail your sources and explain how you decided to use them. It may be that the nature of your work strongly determines particular sources.

Interpretation

- What are examples of current and likely future information requirements?
- Are the sources people or paper-based?
- Are they internal or external sources?
- How do you ensure the reliability of your sources?
- Do you select from a variety of reliable sources?

Candidate illustration

Event route
Rosie drew evidence from a project she undertook to design a guide for volunteer fundraisers that would act as an induction booklet on their appointment. Her sources included research into the expectations of prospective volunteers, organisational policies and procedures, support available and fundraising techniques. She drew from a wide range of established sources and compared the expectations of the prospective volunteers with those of experienced volunteers to ensure that the information was useful.

Event route
Callum was able to cross-reference to the evidence used in Element C5.1, PC (a), where he had to alter shift patterns to accommodate an increase in orders. The information he needed included customer orders, production times and the increase in numbers needed. These sources were mainly internal, but also included the orders received from customers. Callum clearly explained his actions in his analysis of evidence.

Ideas for evidence

- Any information gathered.
- Personal statement indicating sources of the above, and
- Explanations as to why the information was used.
- Witness testimony from those concerned.

Your ideas for evidence

Description of evidence	Location of evidence	Opportunities for cross-referencing	Reflection and analysis

K&U links

Suggested reading for knowledge and understanding purposes:

Cole, G.A., *Management: Theory and Practice,* 5th edition, chapters 19 and 28, pp. 227–8.

Mullins, L.J., *Management and Organisational Behaviour,* 4th edition, chapter 2, pp. 57–8, chapter 9, pp. 292–305.

Needham, D. et al., *Business for Higher Awards,* chapters 9, 26, 27 and 28.

Cross-referencing

This element could be cross-referenced to any unit, depending on the nature of the evidence selected.

	Obtain information for decision making
Element **D4.1**	# Obtain information for decision making

Performance Criterion

(c) *Your methods of obtaining information are reliable, effective and make efficient use of resources.*

> We suggest that you read ahead to PC (d), which will assist with this performance criterion. Make sure that you explain your methods of obtaining information in detail. Methods must include at least four of the following: listening and watching, reading, spoken questioning, written questioning, formal research you have undertaken and/or formal research conducted by others. Detail why your methods were appropriate and illustrate how they made the best use of resources in terms of people, time, budget and materials.

Interpretation

▪ How do you obtain the information that you need?

▪ Does the nature of the information dictate your collection methods?

▪ Is the information qualitative or quantitative?

▪ How do you assure that your methods are reliable?

Candidate illustration

Event route
Val continued using the budgetary allocation events for this element. She detailed the information required: quantitative as amounts of money previously allocated to budget headings and projected for the coming financial year, and qualitative as the department's priorities for service development. She evidenced examples of this information and used written correspondence to show how some of it had been requested. In addition, Val included personal notes of verbal questions she had asked of the finance section and her manager. A personal statement detailed why her approach was appropriate and cost-effective.

Event route
Kieron also continued to use evidence originally referenced in PC (a). Kieron's methods included contacting the embassies of several European countries for information on trading and employment requirements; meetings with experts in the area; the local Business Link; and reading up on the subject in the local university library. Kieron's timescales were tight and he had to obtain the correct information as quickly as possible. This was explained in his analysis. Evidence relating to his methods, meetings, questioning, reading and research on competitors was highlighted through notes, minutes, reading references and research sources, and justified with a personal statement.

Ideas for evidence

■ Evidence sources (may be apparent from the information itself).

■ Personal statement justifying sources.

■ Witness testimony from those involved.

Your ideas for evidence

Description of evidence	Location of evidence	Opportunities for cross-referencing	Reflection and analysis

K&U links

Suggested reading for knowledge and understanding purposes:

Cole, G.A., *Management: Theory and Practice,* 5th edition, chapters 19 and 28, pp. 227–8.

Mullins, L.J., *Management and Organisational Behaviour,* 4th edition, chapter 2, pp. 57–8, chapter 9, pp. 292–305.

Needham, D. et al., *Business for Higher Awards,* chapters 9, 26, 27 and 28.

Cross-referencing

This element could be cross-referenced to any unit, depending on the nature of the evidence selected.

Element D4.1   Obtain information for decision making

Performance Criterion

(d) Your methods of obtaining information are consistent with organisational values, policies and legal requirements.

Clearly, these methods can be directly cross-referenced from the previous PC. Your analysis should identify the organisational and legal requirements that impact on your methods of information gathering.

Interpretation

◼ How do organisational requirements and values inform on acceptable methods of obtaining information?

◼ Which legal requirements have you complied with?

Candidate illustration

Event route

Both Val and Kieron were able to cross-reference to PC (c). Val highlighted the council requirements relating to confidentiality, and treasury guidelines relating to financial analysis. Kieron highlighted the European Union export and trading legislation that impacted on his strategy and explained how he complied with it.

Ideas for evidence

◼ Personal statement explaining compliance with organisational and legal requirements.

◼ Cross-reference to PC (c).

◼ Copies of relevant organisational and legal requirements.

Your ideas for evidence

Description of evidence	Location of evidence	Opportunities for cross-referencing	Reflection and analysis

K&U links

Suggested reading for knowledge and understanding purposes:

Cole, G.A., *Management: Theory and Practice*, 5th edition, chapters 19 and 28, pp. 227–8.

Mullins, L.J., *Management and Organisational Behaviour*, 4th edition, chapter 2, pp. 57–8, chapter 9, pp. 292–305.

Needham, D. et al., *Business for Higher Awards*, chapters 9, 26, 27 and 28.

Cross-referencing

This element could be cross-referenced to any unit, depending on the nature of the evidence selected.

Element D4.1 Obtain information for decision making

Performance Criterion

(e) *The information you obtain is accurate, relevant and sufficient to support decision making.*

> If you are using the event route, you will be able to cross-reference to existing evidence. Your analysis should explain your methods of confirming that the information obtained is accurate and reliable. Make sure you detail your actions confirming this.

Interpretation

▌ What are the consequences if information is inaccurate or irrelevant?

▌ How do you avoid this and ensure that decision making is based on relevant, sufficient, accurate information?

Candidate illustration

Event route
Rosie continued to focus on her guidebook project (see PC (b)). In a personal statement she explained how she tried to triangulate her findings from prospective volunteers against those of existing volunteers. In this way she ensured that information was relevant for her purposes.

Event route
The information that Callum obtained in preparation for changing shift patterns (see PC (b)) was confirmed through discussions with internal sources and through conversations with his line manager. Testimonies from sources were obtained in support of the cross-referenced evidence.

Ideas for evidence

▌ Personal statement explaining compilation methods.

▌ Witness testimony from those involved.

▌ Cross-references to examples of information.

Your ideas for evidence

Description of evidence	Location of evidence	Opportunities for cross-referencing	Reflection and analysis

K&U links

Suggested reading for knowledge and understanding purposes:

Cole, G.A., *Management: Theory and Practice,* 5th edition, chapters 19 and 28, pp. 227–8.

Mullins, L.J., *Management and Organisational Behaviour,* 4th edition, chapter 2, pp. 57–8, chapter 9, pp. 292–305.

Needham, D. et al., *Business for Higher Awards,* chapters 9, 26, 27 and 28.

Cross-referencing

This element could be cross-referenced to any unit, depending on the nature of the evidence selected.

Element D4.1   Obtain information for decision making

Performance Criterion

(f) Where information is inadequate, contradictory or ambiguous, you take prompt and effective action to deal with this.

> Your evidence, reflection and analysis should explain an instance where information you had was inaccurate in some way. Detail the incident and illustrate how you obtained alternative information or clarified existing information.

Interpretation

◼ How do you identify inaccuracy in information?

◼ Does the nature of the problem dictate your actions?

◼ What actions are taken?

◼ What was the outcome?

Candidate illustration

Event route

During her analysis of previous expenditure, Val found that there were inaccuracies in the figures provided, as the total amount of expenditure did not equal the amount of expenditure indicated under each cost heading. She explained this error in her analysis and evidenced written communication sent to the finance section requesting an explanation. She also included the reply, which indicated that additional ancillary costs were included in the total expenditure. She was provided with a breakdown of these costs.

Event route

Kieron continued to use the export strategy for evidence. He was concerned that some of the information on legislation he had obtained was now obsolete because of changes in European Union trading and UK Customs and Excise duty laws. Kieron sought clarification from the Internet, since it provided the most up-to-date information. He found that several fine details regarding export and import licences and duty had changed. He printed off the information and included it as evidence, together with a personal statement explaining his actions.

Ideas for evidence

◼ Cross-reference to existing evidence, if taking the event route.

◼ Detail your actions with further performance evidence, if available.

◼ Personal statement explaining circumstances.

◼ Witness testimony from others involved.

◼ Correspondence sent and received.

◼ Email and Internet printouts.

Your ideas for evidence

Description of evidence	Location of evidence	Opportunities for cross-referencing	Reflection and analysis

K&U links

Suggested reading for knowledge and understanding purposes:

Cole, G.A., *Management: Theory and Practice,* 5th edition, chapters 19 and 28, pp. 227–8.

Mullins, L.J., *Management and Organisational Behaviour,* 4th edition, chapter 2, pp. 57–8, chapter 9, pp. 292–305.

Needham, D. et al., *Business for Higher Awards,* chapters 9, 26, 27 and 28.

Cross-referencing

This element could be cross-referenced to any unit, depending on the nature of the evidence selected.

Element D4.2   **Record and store information**

Performance Criterion

(a) *Your systems and procedures for recording and storing information are suitable for the purpose and make efficient use of resources.*

> This PC will require you to explain your recording systems and illustrate why they are suitable. Don't forget to detail how you operate your record system.

Interpretation

▌ Are the systems you use specific to you and your team, or are they organisation-wide?

▌ Does your role and the nature of the information involved dictate recording and storage methods?

Candidate illustration

Event route
Val focused on client files and the storage of confidential information in compliance with organisational requirements. She drew a plan of her office areas explaining where documents were stored and the security measures in place. Her assessor was familiar with Val's office as she had already conducted an on-site assessment (see Unit C5, Element C5.3, PC (g)), and so Val also cross-referenced to the observational assessment document her assessor had given her.

Callum did not use many paper-based documents and stored the majority of his qualitative and quantitative information on computer hard drives and floppy disks. His system involved backing up all information on floppy disk to ensure that no files were lost or deleted. For evidence, Callum included computer-generated printouts of databases used to store statistical information and a personal statement explaining his back-up system.

Ideas for evidence

▌ Plan or map of office layout and storage systems (your assessor can be invited to observe your office and storage system if required).

▌ Printouts of computer-based storage systems.

▌ Personal statement explaining system.

Your ideas for evidence

Description of evidence	Location of evidence	Opportunities for cross-referencing	Reflection and analysis

K&U links

Suggested reading for knowledge and understanding purposes:

Cole, G.A., *Management: Theory and Practice*, 5th edition, chapter 26.

Mullins, L.J., *Management and Organisational Behaviour*, 4th edition, chapter 2, pp. 57–8, chapter 9, pp. 292–305.

Needham, D. et al., *Business for Higher Awards*, chapters 9, 26, 27 and 28.

Cross-referencing

This element could be cross-referenced to any unit, depending on the nature of the evidence selected.

Element D4.2   Record and store information

Performance Criterion

(b) *The way you record and store information complies with organisational policies and procedures.*

> You will need to explain the actions you take in recording and storing information. Detail the procedures that impact on your actions. Policies and procedures may be concerned with access, retrieval, confidentiality and information systems.

Interpretation

■ How do you record and store information?

■ Which policies and procedures inform on recording and storage of information?

■ Are these formal or informal?

■ How do you interpret them in action to ensure compliance?

Candidate illustration

Event route
Rosie illustrated her competence by focusing on the organisation-wide information database. This required regular input from managers concerning client, staff and training information. A routine part of her role was to provide the information system with details of sickness and absenteeism. For evidence, Rosie included printouts of the database and an explanation of input methods. Paper-based documentation was also included as the basis for input onto the computerised system.

Kieron based his evidence on the recording of financial information. This information projected turnover based on sales in particular months. Kieron's organisation used an off-the-shelf management accounting package for this purpose. Kieron also used sales figures obtained from the sales force as raw data evidence and the results of inputting onto the computerised management accounting system. He obtained a testimony from the accounting section confirming the use of the accounting package across the organisation.

Ideas for evidence

■ Printouts from computerised storage and retrieval systems.

■ Examples of paper-based systems.

■ Personal statement.

■ Witness testimony.

Your ideas for evidence

Description of evidence	Location of evidence	Opportunities for cross-referencing	Reflection and analysis

K&U links

Suggested reading for knowledge and understanding purposes:

Cole, G.A., *Management: Theory and Practice,* 5th edition, chapter 26.

Mullins, L.J., *Management and Organisational Behaviour,* 4th edition, chapter 2, pp. 57–8, chapter 9, pp. 292–305.

Needham, D. et al., *Business for Higher Awards,* chapters 9, 26, 27 and 28.

Cross-referencing

This element could be cross-referenced to any unit, depending on the nature of the evidence selected.

Element D4.2 Record and store information

Performance Criterion

(c) The information you record and store is readily accessible in the required format to authorised people only.

> You will need to explain your methods of access to computer-based and paper-based information. Detail the reasons behind particular access formats and say why they are appropriate.

Interpretation

- Who can access particular items of information?

- How is access restricted and controlled?

- Does the nature of the information dictate formats for storage and presentation?

Candidate illustration

Event route
Val continued to focus on client records (see PC (a)). These involved individual service requirements and delivery plans agreed with each client which were updated by the people involved following regular review of service requirements. Standardised documentation was used for this purpose, which formed the basis of Val's evidence. Access was limited to those involved with individual clients and was controlled by a records and filing officer who was directly supervised by Val. Val obtained a testimony from the officer confirming the system employed.

Event route
Rosie drew evidence from her involvement with the organisation-wide database (see PC (b)). Access to particular parts of the database was password-protected. Rosie invited her assessor to observe her accessing information and explained the formatting of information during noted discussions with her assessor. Notes of questions and answers were included as evidence and confirmed by Rosie's assessor.

Ideas for evidence

- Examples of paper-based documentation used.

- Personal statement explaining formatting of information.

- Personal statement, witness testimony or observation by your assessor confirming accessibility arrangements for substantive or confidential information.

Your ideas for evidence

Description of evidence	Location of evidence	Opportunities for cross-referencing	Reflection and analysis

K&U links

Suggested reading for knowledge and understanding purposes:

Cole, G.A., *Management: Theory and Practice*, 5th edition, chapter 26.

Mullins, L.J., *Management and Organisational Behaviour*, 4th edition, chapter 2, pp. 57–8, chapter 9, pp. 292–305.

Needham, D. et al., *Business for Higher Awards*, chapters 9, 26, 27 and 28.

Cross-referencing

This element could be cross-referenced to any unit, depending on the nature of the evidence selected.

Element D4.2 Record and store information

Performance Criterion

(d) You provide opportunities for team members to make suggestions for improvements to systems and procedures.

To meet the requirements of this PC you will need to illustrate your competence by using a specific incident or event in which your staff have made suggestions for improvements to information recording and storage systems.

Interpretation

▪ How are opportunities provided?

▪ Are systems regularly reviewed?

▪ In what way are suggestions made?

Candidate illustration

Event route

Val's organisation operated a staff suggestion scheme, which began at local team level with suggestions being discussed and agreed. These were then passed to a review panel comprising middle and senior management. Val's team had had several suggestions regarding confidentiality. Val used examples of suggestions and correspondence with the review panel as evidence.

Kieron regularly invited suggestions for improvements from his sales team during team meetings. Many suggestions had been made and implemented concerning the point at which a sale had been made. The issues revolved around verbal agreements and contracts, delivery notes, invoices and faulty products. The team did not have a standardised method for recording sales, and this was resolved through discussion at a particular team meeting and detailed in the minutes. Kieron also drew up a systems diagram detailing the changes made to improve accuracy of sales information.

Ideas for evidence

▪ Examples of staff suggestions.

▪ Outcomes of suggestions made.

▪ Notes of discussions.

▪ Minutes of meetings.

▪ Witness testimony from staff involved.

▪ Representations of improvements made.

Your ideas for evidence

Description of evidence	Location of evidence	Opportunities for cross-referencing	Reflection and analysis

K&U links

Suggested reading for knowledge and understanding purposes:

Cole, G.A., *Management: Theory and Practice,* 5th edition, chapter 26.

Mullins, L.J., *Management and Organisational Behaviour,* 4th edition, chapter 2, pp. 57–8, chapter 9, pp. 292–305.

Needham, D. et al., *Business for Higher Awards,* chapters 9, 26, 27 and 28.

Cross-referencing

This element could be cross-referenced to any unit, depending on the nature of the evidence selected.

Element D4.2 Record and store information

Performance Criterion

(e) *You made recommendations for improvements to systems and procedures to the relevant people.*

> Clearly, this can be linked to PC (c). Explain your role in making suggestions for improvements. Detail the circumstances in which suggestions were made. Highlight who the relevant people were.

Interpretation

▌ Under what circumstances have you made recommendations?

▌ Who are the relevant people?

Candidate illustration

Event route
Val detailed her involvement with the staff suggestion scheme at the review stage (see PC (d)). She explained how suggestions were forwarded to the review panel. This procedure was evidenced using correspondence with the panel.

Event route
Callum submitted a written report that evaluated the storage and analysis of production line quality assurance information. The project was part of his management training programme and suggestions were made to his line manager in a verbal presentation. Overhead transparencies from the presentation and a personal statement were also submitted.

Ideas for evidence

▌ Correspondence concerning your suggestions.

▌ Written reports.

▌ Details of presentations made.

▌ Personal statement detailing events.

▌ Witness testimony from the appropriate people.

Your ideas for evidence

Description of evidence	Location of evidence	Opportunities for cross-referencing	Reflection and analysis

K&U links

Suggested reading for knowledge and understanding purposes:

Cole, G.A., *Management: Theory and Practice,* 5th edition, chapter 26.

Mullins, L.J., *Management and Organisational Behaviour,* 4th edition, chapter 2, pp. 57–8, chapter 9, pp. 292–305.

Needham, D. et al., *Business for Higher Awards,* chapters 9, 26, 27 and 28.

Cross-referencing

This element could be cross-referenced to any unit, depending on the nature of the evidence selected.

Element D4.2 Record and store information

Performance Criterion

(f) *Your recommendations take account of organisational constraints.*

> You can cross-reference to existing evidence, if appropriate, but make sure you explain the constraints on particular suggestions made.

Interpretation

▮ What is the nature of organisational constraints?

▮ Are they due to policy, procedures, resources or anything else?

Candidate illustration

Event route
Val regularly discussed possible constraints at the review stage of the staff suggestion scheme (see PC (e)). Examples of constraints, and the discussions around them, were part of the minutes of the review meetings. Relevant sections were highlighted and submitted as evidence.

Event route
Callum cross-referenced to the report evidenced for PC (e). Constraints on his proposals for storage and analysis of production line quality assurance information related to the timely availability of the information. In turn, availability of information was limited by organisational procedures for quality assurance monitoring, which did not stipulate timescales between monitoring proposals. This made information flows sporadic. Callum's recommendations advocated pre-planned, appropriate times for quality assurance monitoring to occur.

Ideas for evidence

▮ Cross-reference to existing evidence.

▮ Written reports detailing recommendations and likely constraints.

▮ Minutes of meetings.

▮ Correspondence.

▮ Personal statements.

Your ideas for evidence

Description of evidence	Location of evidence	Opportunities for cross-referencing	Reflection and analysis

K&U links

Suggested reading for knowledge and understanding purposes:

Cole, G.A., *Management: Theory and Practice,* 5th edition, chapter 26.

Mullins, L.J., *Management and Organisational Behaviour,* 4th edition, chapter 2, pp. 57–8, chapter 9, pp. 292–305.

Needham, D. et al., *Business for Higher Awards,* chapters 9, 26, 27 and 28.

Cross-referencing

This element could be cross-referenced to any unit, depending on the nature of the evidence selected.

Element D4.3	**Analyse information to support decision making**

Performance Criterion

(a) You identify objectives for your analysis which are clear and consistent with the decisions which need to be made.

> You will need to evidence specific objectives for your analysis of information. Detail how they were compiled and their relevance to the decisions to be made.

Interpretation

■ How are the outcomes of analysis formed into objectives?

■ How do the nature of the decisions to be made impact on the objectives of your analysis?

■ How do you ensure that your objectives support decision making?

Candidate illustration

Event route
Callum cross-referenced to his quality assurance monitoring and information recording project originally referenced for Element D4.2, PC (e). The report was based on analysis of statistical information and the time taken to make statistics relating to quality assurance monitoring available. His objectives were clearly stated in the report and self-explanatory – they supported the purpose of the report, which was to ensure that the monitoring of products coming off the production line was accurate and timely. This was clearly explained in a personal statement.

Event route
Val again returned to her role in the staff suggestions scheme (see Element D4.2, PC (d)). She detailed the objectives set out by her team when analysing information about staff suggestions before passing them on to the review panel. Analysis occurred through discussion of the ideas, implications, constraints and benefits to be derived. Minutes of the meetings and witness testimony from two of the team members involved were submitted as evidence.

Ideas for evidence

■ Written objectives for analysis of information.

■ Minutes of meetings.

■ Extracts from reports.

■ Personal statement explaining actions.

■ Witness testimony from others involved.

Your ideas for evidence

Description of evidence	Location of evidence	Opportunities for cross-referencing	Reflection and analysis

K&U links

Suggested reading for knowledge and understanding purposes:

Cole, G.A., *Management: Theory and Practice,* 5th edition, chapter 19.

Mullins, L.J., *Management and Organisational Behaviour,* 4th edition, chapter 9.

Needham, D. et al., *Business for Higher Awards,* chapters 9, 26, 27 and 28.

Cross-referencing

This element could be cross-referenced to any unit, depending on the nature of the evidence selected.

Element D4.3 | Analyse information to support decision making

Performance Criterion

(b) You select information which is accurate, relevant to the objectives and sufficient to arrive at reliable decisions.

Make sure you link to Elements D4.1 and D4.2 (if relevant). Clearly explain the nature of the information that you are analysing and detail why it is appropriate.

Interpretation

▌ Which parts of your job require you to analyse information?

▌ Why do you analyse this information? What is the outcome of this analysis?

▌ How does this inform you as to what information is needed?

Candidate illustration

Event route
Kieron detailed his routine responsibilities concerning after-sales customer services. His company provided extensive on-site services to businesses and individual clients. Kieron explained that he regularly monitored qualitative and quantitative information on customer requirements, faulty products and maintenance queries so that he could identify trends in customer requirements, product line faults and the use made of the company's range of optional after-sales services. The information was analysed and used to identify improvements to products and changes to on-site services in line with customers' requirements. Kieron regularly obtained the information from the customer service team and collated and analysed it using a computer-based package to pinpoint trends and common customer requirements. Findings and recommendations were fed into management meetings and strategic and tactical work groups. Kieron used the reports submitted to management and working groups, highlighting the information used, together with a witness testimony clarifying his actions from his manager, the managing director.

Event route
Rosie concentrated on an informal, non-routine piece of work that she had undertaken for her organisation. The work was needed to identify methods for applying for donations from a lottery's charity board. Rosie initially contacted the board to obtain the documentation and guidance notes supplied, then made use of her contacts in other charitable and non-profit-making organisations to find out how they had applied so that she could learn about the process. She used correspondence with those involved and her replies as evidence of selecting accurate and relevant information.

Ideas for evidence

- Reports detailing information and objectives.
- Personal statement explaining circumstances.
- Witness testimony from those involved.
- Examples of information obtained.
- Correspondence concerning information.

Your ideas for evidence

Description of evidence	Location of evidence	Opportunities for cross-referencing	Reflection and analysis

K&U links

Suggested reading for knowledge and understanding purposes:

Cole, G.A., *Management: Theory and Practice,* 5th edition, chapter 19.

Mullins, L.J., *Management and Organisational Behaviour,* 4th edition, chapter 9.

Needham, D. et al., *Business for Higher Awards,* chapters 9, 26, 27 and 28.

Cross-referencing

This element could be cross-referenced to any unit, depending on the nature of the evidence selected.

Element D4.3   Analyse information to support decision making

Performance Criterion

(c) You use methods of analysis which are suitable to achieve the objectives.

You can link to previous evidence and analysis, if appropriate. Explain your methods of analysing information.

Interpretation

■ How do the objectives dictate methods of analysis?

■ Which methods of analysis were used?

■ Are alternative methods considered and used, if appropriate?

■ Are methods formal and planned, or informal and ad hoc?

■ Does your analysis involve qualitative and quantitative information?

Candidate illustration

Event route

Callum continued focusing on the quality assurance work he was undertaking (see PC (a)). He explained that his analysis of information had initially been quantitative, plotting timescales against the number of products monitored for quality. He undertook further qualitative research by meeting with those involved in the quality assurance process to explain his findings. Examples of the information analysed, in the form of bar charts and diagrams, were used as evidence, together with notes of discussions with those involved.

Event route

Val received a letter from the finance section requesting information and an explanation of the rising car mileage claims made by members of her team. She had routinely monitored car mileage claims and had already noticed a steady rise in claims from all staff, herself included. Val brought the issue to the next team meeting and requested information from her team on their journeys and reasons for travelling. Val decided to undertake a cost–benefit analysis of mileage claims against services provided based on this information. She detailed a representative sample of journeys and justification for each one against the costs incurred. Her analysis, which consisted mostly of reading the information to pick out key trends and issues, identified that journeys had become longer and more frequent because of the expansion of her team's geographical area of responsibility. Her evidence consisted of the report forwarded to the finance department, together with her rough notes made during analysis of the information.

Ideas for evidence	▮ Evidence of analysis; information plotted in diagrammatic form, summary of findings.
	▮ Reports.
	▮ Minutes of meetings.
	▮ Notes of discussions.
	▮ Personal statement explaining findings and context.
	▮ Witness testimony from those involved.

Your ideas for evidence

Description of evidence	Location of evidence	Opportunities for cross-referencing	Reflection and analysis

K&U links

Suggested reading for knowledge and understanding purposes:

Cole, G.A., *Management: Theory and Practice,* 5th edition, chapter 19.

Mullins, L.J., *Management and Organisational Behaviour,* 4th edition, chapter 9.

Needham, D. et al., *Business for Higher Awards,* chapters 9, 26, 27 and 28.

Cross-referencing

This element could be cross-referenced to any unit, depending on the nature of the evidence selected.

Element D4.3   Analyse information to support decision making

Performance Criterion

(d) Your analysis of the information correctly identifies relevant patterns and trends.

Use any opportunity to cross-reference, if relevant. Highlight patterns and trends in the information you have analysed, and explain their significance.

Interpretation

▌ In the context of the work that you do, what kinds of patterns and trends in information are relevant?

▌ What are patterns and trends used for?

▌ How are these identified?

Candidate illustration

Event route
Val focused on the trends in car mileage claims (see PC (c)) and detailed that they had risen because of increased and extended journeys. She highlighted this section of her report to the finance department as evidence.

Event route
Kieron also highlighted trends in changing customer requirements regarding after-sales service and support (see PC (b)). This significant finding required the company to review the range of services it offered. He highlighted this part of his report to the management team and included a personal statement explaining the implications for customer services.

Ideas for evidence

▌ Details of trends and patterns:
  – reports;
  – presentations;
  – statistical output.

▌ Personal statement explaining implications.

▌ Notes of findings.

Your ideas for evidence

Description of evidence	Location of evidence	Opportunities for cross-referencing	Reflection and analysis

K&U links   Suggested reading for knowledge and understanding purposes:

Cole, G.A., *Management: Theory and Practice,* 5th edition, chapter 19.

Mullins, L.J., *Management and Organisational Behaviour,* 4th edition, chapter 9.

Needham, D. et al., *Business for Higher Awards,* chapters 9, 26, 27 and 28.

Cross-referencing   This element could be cross-referenced to any unit, depending on the nature of the evidence selected.

Element D4.3 Analyse information to support decision making

Performance Criterion

(e) You support your conclusions with reasoned argument and appropriate evidence.

> To meet the requirements of this PC, you will need to explain how your conclusions are based on the results of your analysis and are objective and justified. Detail the process of drawing conclusions from the implications of your analysis.

Interpretation

- How do you draw conclusions?
- How are these justified?
- How is your reasoning communicated to others?

Candidate illustration

Event route
Callum simply highlighted the conclusions section of his report concerning quality assurance monitoring (see PC (c)). His conclusions were clearly based on factual information which indicated that monitoring did not occur in a planned and structured way, which meant that easily solved product faults were not dealt with before distribution. In addition, Callum obtained a witness testimony from his line manager confirming his conclusions and methods of drawing them.

Event route
Val's conclusions regarding car mileage claims (see PC (c)) were also clearly based on her analysis of factual information. Her conclusions were that mileage claims had increased due to staff being required to cover greater distances. She highlighted the section of her report to the finance department and included some of the information obtained from staff regarding journeys made.

Ideas for evidence

- Cross-reference to existing evidence, if appropriate.
- Extracts from reports highlighting conclusions.
- Evidence of conclusions being linked to findings following analysis, for example summaries of findings.
- Examples of information on which conclusions were based.
- Witness testimony from others involved.
- Personal statement explaining circumstances and actions.

Your ideas for evidence

Description of evidence	Location of evidence	Opportunities for cross-referencing	Reflection and analysis

K&U links   Suggested reading for knowledge and understanding purposes:

Cole, G.A., *Management: Theory and Practice,* 5th edition, chapter 19.

Mullins, L.J., *Management and Organisational Behaviour,* 4th edition, chapter 9.

Needham, D. et al., *Business for Higher Awards,* chapters 9, 26, 27 and 28.

Cross-referencing   This element could be cross-referenced to any unit, depending on the nature of the evidence selected.

Element D4.3   Analyse information to support decision making

**Performance
Criterion**

*(f) In presenting the results of your analysis you differentiate clearly
between fact and opinion.*

> You will need to detail how you clarify results, cross-referencing to
> existing evidence if appropriate. It may be that conclusions and
> recommendations are made separately to draw distinctions between
> fact and opinion.

Interpretation

- How is the analysis of information presented?
- Is there a difference between results, conclusions and
recommendations?
- How are these presented?

**Candidate
illustration**

Event route
Kieron again used his report regarding after-sales customer services
as evidence (see PC (b)). The report was formal and clearly presented
the findings of the research. Recommendations were made
separately, enabling Kieron to make a distinction between the factual
aspects of the conclusions and his opinion (recommendations).

Event route
Val also cross-referenced to her report regarding car mileage claims
(see PC (c)). The report ended with a summary and explanation of
findings. As a consequence of her report, Val suggested changes to the
car mileage claim form completed by staff. In her recommendations,
Val referenced her report to justify the need to supply the finance
department with more detail regarding the purpose of journeys
made. Her opinion was that this would provide ongoing justification
for any increase in claims.

Ideas for evidence

- Cross-reference to existing evidence, if appropriate.
- Details of reports that make a clear distinction between fact and
opinion.
- Additional written recommendations, or records of verbal
recommendations, minutes of meetings.
- Correspondence.

Your ideas for evidence

Description of evidence	Location of evidence	Opportunities for cross-referencing	Reflection and analysis

K&U links

Suggested reading for knowledge and understanding purposes:

Cole, G.A., *Management: Theory and Practice,* 5th edition, chapter 19.

Mullins, L.J., *Management and Organisational Behaviour,* 4th edition, chapter 9.

Needham, D. et al., *Business for Higher Awards,* chapters 9, 26, 27 and 28.

Cross-referencing

This element could be cross-referenced to any unit, depending on the nature of the evidence selected.

Element D4.3 Analyse information to support decision making

Performance Criterion

(g) *Your records of analysis are sufficient to show the assumptions and decisions made at each stage.*

Detail, with evidence, the justifications for your assumptions and decisions. These may already be included in your existing evidence. Highlight the examples of records of qualitative and quantitative analysis of information.

Interpretation

■ What records are kept?

■ Are any assumptions and/or decisions made clear?

■ How do you justify your conclusions and recommendations?

Candidate illustration

Event route
Callum continued using his work regarding quality assurance monitoring on the production line (see PC (e)). He submitted examples of the computer-based conclusions that were made in order to present his findings in diagram form. He also included a personal statement linking the raw information with the collated results. This demonstrated any assumptions or decisions he had made about the information he was working from.

Event route
Rosie cross-referenced to her correspondence with external colleagues regarding an application for a lottery grant (see PC (b)). In some cases she noticed conflicting or contradictory advice. She decided to treat some of it with scepticism since she realised that, although they were colleagues, they may all be competing for the same money. She explained this in her report and highlighted examples of where she had used her discretion.

Ideas for evidence

■ Cross-reference to existing evidence, if appropriate.

■ Extracts from reports.

■ Personal statement explaining actions.

■ Correspondence.

■ Examples of records kept.

Your ideas for evidence

Description of evidence	Location of evidence	Opportunities for cross-referencing	Reflection and analysis

K&U links

Suggested reading for knowledge and understanding purposes:

Cole, G.A., *Management: Theory and Practice,* 5th edition, chapter 19.

Mullins, L.J., *Management and Organisational Behaviour,* 4th edition, chapter 9.

Needham, D. et al., *Business for Higher Awards,* chapters 9, 26, 27 and 28.

Cross-referencing

This element could be cross-referenced to any unit, depending on the nature of the evidence selected.

Element D4.4 Advise and inform others

Performance Criterion

(a) *You research the advice and information needs of your recipients in ways which are appropriate and sufficient and take account of your organisational constraints.*

> Detail specific instances where you have advised and informed staff, peers, senior managers or external colleagues and customers. This may be upon request or on your own initiative. Focus on how you sought clarification on what these people required of you. Explain how organisational constraints such as policy and procedures and the availability of resources impacted on how you identified their information needs.

Interpretation

▌ Under what circumstances have you had to research the information needs of others?

▌ How was this achieved?

▌ What type of organisational constraints did you have to work within?

Candidate illustration

Event route
Kieron was able to cross-reference to his report to senior managers on customers' after-sales service requirements (see Element D4.3, PC (b)). Kieron defined senior managers as recipients for the purpose of this element and highlighted how he had been asked to identify trends or patterns in customer requirements to enable the company to continue meeting their needs. Given this remit, Kieron met with his line manager, the managing director, to clarify what the senior management team required. He took notes of this meeting to help him with his work and submitted them as evidence, together with a witness testimony from the managing director. In his analysis, Kieron fully explained the significance of the work he was undertaking and the impact it would have on the company. In this case, the organisational constraint within which Kieron was working was identified as the information systems from which he gathered the information.

Event route
Rosie also continued using the work she had done on applying for a national lottery grant (see Element D4.3, PC (b)). As the application would be the first of its kind made by her organisation, she was aware that procedures and guidelines would have to be established to enable subsequent applications to be made. Through discussion with colleagues and senior managers, she identified that the best way to do this was to provide specimen copies of completed application documentation as an example, together with guidance notes for managers making applications. Rosie explained the impact on policy and procedures in a personal statement and submitted notes taken during discussions with others regarding the application process.

Ideas for evidence

- Notes of conversations.
- Minutes of meetings.
- Cross-reference to other evidence, if appropriate.
- Personal statement.
- Witness testimony.
- Correspondence.

Your ideas for evidence

Description of evidence	Location of evidence	Opportunities for cross-referencing	Reflection and analysis

K&U links

Suggested reading for knowledge and understanding purposes:

Cole, G.A., *Management: Theory and Practice,* 5th edition, chapters 19 and 26.

Mullins, L.J., *Management and Organisational Behaviour,* 4th edition, chapter 9.

Needham, D. et al., *Business for Higher Awards,* chapters 9, 26, 27 and 28.

Cross-referencing

This element could be cross-referenced to any unit, depending on the nature of the evidence selected.

Element D4.4 Advise and inform others

Performance Criterion

(b) You provide advice and information at a time and place and in a form and manner appropriate to the needs of your recipients.

> You should concentrate on a specific example where you have provided advice and information. Focus on how it was provided and why this was appropriate considering your audience and the nature of the information.

Interpretation

■ When providing information, how do you ensure that it is communicated in the most appropriate way?

■ Do the nature and significance of the information dictate methods of communication?

■ Who is your potential audience? Do they impact on how and where information is communicated?

Candidate illustration

Event route
Kieron focused on the introduction of a new product to the sales team, who would be demonstrating it to potential customers. He summoned the entire sales force to a meeting to explain the features and benefits of the product, together with technical specifications and prices. The event combined written information with a visual demonstration of the product, a short presentation by Kieron, and a technical explanation from one of the production team. The sales team received handouts containing detailed information, and were invited to examine and use the product and to ask questions of Kieron and the technical expert he had invited. As evidence, Kieron submitted examples of the handouts and overhead transparencies from his presentation. He annotated these, explaining how the technical data contained in the handouts would need to act as a reference for sales staff until they became familiar with the product. He also included a personal statement explaining the benefits to staff of having hands-on experience of new products before their introduction in the marketplace.

Event route
Rosie was able to cross-reference to a previous unit, where she had produced guidelines for fundraising activities aimed at volunteers (see Unit A4, Element A4.1, PC (b)). The guidelines were produced following a request from volunteer fundraisers. Rosie decided to produce a booklet that would enable volunteers to identify their own methods and link with organisational procedures and objectives. These were listed in an applied and practical way in the booklet. In addition to the booklet, Rosie submitted a personal statement explaining that she did not want to standardise the ways in which funds were raised as this would limit ideas and creativity. She also ensured that the guidelines were available in minority languages and on cassette in order to maintain the equal opportunity policies of her organisation.

Ideas for evidence

∎ Examples of information provided.

∎ Explanations of why it was appropriate to the needs of recipients.

∎ Personal statement.

∎ Witness testimony from those involved.

∎ Details of timescales and their significance.

Your ideas for evidence

Description of evidence	Location of evidence	Opportunities for cross-referencing	Reflection and analysis

K&U links

Suggested reading for knowledge and understanding purposes:

Cole, G.A., *Management: Theory and Practice,* 5th edition, chapters 19 and 26.

Mullins, L.J., *Management and Organisational Behaviour,* 4th edition, chapter 9.

Needham, D. et al., *Business for Higher Awards,* chapters 9, 26, 27 and 28.

Cross-referencing

This element could be cross-referenced to any unit, depending on the nature of the evidence selected.

Element D4.4 Advise and inform others

Performance Criterion

(c) *The information you provide is accurate, current, relevant and significant.*

> Focus on specific items or events and explain how you have ensured that the information is technically correct, up-to-date, useful and provided in the right amount of depth for recipients.

Interpretation

■ How do you ensure the above?

■ Does the nature of the information and your knowledge of the recipients dictate the levels of accuracy and sufficiency needed?

Candidate illustration

Event route
Both Kieron and Rosie were able to cross-reference to PC (b) and highlight examples of the information provided that meet the requirements here. In addition, Kieron obtained a witness testimony from the member of the production team who produced the technical information to confirm accuracy, currency, relevancy and sufficiency of detail.

Ideas for evidence

■ Cross-reference to previous evidence, if appropriate.

■ Witness testimony from others involved confirming the nature of the information.

Your ideas for evidence

Description of evidence	Location of evidence	Opportunities for cross-referencing	Reflection and analysis

K&U links

Suggested reading for knowledge and understanding purposes:

Cole, G.A., *Management: Theory and Practice,* 5th edition, chapters 19 and 26.

Mullins, L.J., *Management and Organisational Behaviour,* 4th edition, chapter 9.

Needham, D. et al., *Business for Higher Awards,* chapters 9, 26, 27 and 28.

Cross-referencing

This element could be cross-referenced to any unit, depending on the nature of the evidence selected.

Element D4.4 Advise and inform others

Performance Criterion

(d) *Your advice is consistent with organisational policy, procedures and constraints.*

> Again, we suggest that you focus on specific examples where you have advised and informed others. Highlight how organisational policies and procedures and the availability of resources have impacted on the advice provided. Explain the implications of this.

Interpretation

■ How do you ensure that any advice given complies with policy, procedure and constraints?

■ Why is this important?

Candidate illustration

Event route

Callum cross-referenced to his work on quality assurance monitoring (see Element D4.2, PC (e)). He highlighted the recommendations for improvement contained in the report, which also identified implications for production line work procedures and the availability of time and human resources to conduct regular quality assurance checks.

Val drew evidence from the induction process used by all managers. Set procedures and policy had to be communicated to all new employees both verbally, with examples of the use of procedures, and in writing as part of the induction handbook. Val submitted evidence of the induction of a new employee into her team and obtained a testimony from her confirming the advice she had given.

Ideas for evidence

■ Cross-reference to existing evidence, if appropriate.

■ Examples of advice given.

■ Detail of organisational implications.

■ Confirmation of actions through witness testimony.

Your ideas for evidence

Description of evidence	Location of evidence	Opportunities for cross-referencing	Reflection and analysis

K&U links

Suggested reading for knowledge and understanding purposes:

Cole, G.A., *Management: Theory and Practice,* 5th edition, chapters 19 and 26.

Mullins, L.J., *Management and Organisational Behaviour,* 4th edition, chapter 9.

Needham, D. et al., *Business for Higher Awards,* chapters 9, 26, 27 and 28.

Cross-referencing

This element could be cross-referenced to any unit, depending on the nature of the evidence selected.

Element D4.4   Advise and inform others

Performance Criterion

(e) *Your advice is supported by reasoned argument and appropriate evidence.*

You should explain how you confirm advice given or justify courses of action and suggestions.

Interpretation

■ Why is it important to be able to justify advice?

■ When have you provided evidence in support of advice?

■ Why has this been necessary?

Candidate illustration

Event route

Rosie was able to cross-reference to her work on lottery grant applications (see PC (a)). Her recommendations from the report were clearly justified through cross-reference to the guidelines provided by the lottery board. In applying the guidelines to her organisation, Rosie clearly justified methods of application, referencing organisational procedures and models of best practice obtained from other organisations. The report and references were cross-referenced as evidence. In her analysis, Rosie clearly explained each item of evidence and its relevance to the requirements of the performance criterion.

Event route

During a review of progress for the new employee undergoing induction (see PC (d)), Val was questioned on the advice she had given about personal information and confidentiality. Val was able to reassure the new employee that while personal information was held on file and on the department's information database, it could not be accessed due to a password-protection system. Val was able to demonstrate the system while the employee observed. Val noted the conversations and included this as evidence, together with a witness testimony from the staff member concerned.

Ideas for evidence

■ Cross-reference to existing evidence, if appropriate.

■ Extracts from reports where recommendations have been justified.

■ Notes of conversations.

■ Formal minutes of meetings.

■ Witness testimony from others involved.

Your ideas for evidence

Description of evidence	Location of evidence	Opportunities for cross-referencing	Reflection and analysis

K&U links   Suggested reading for knowledge and understanding purposes:

Cole, G.A., *Management: Theory and Practice,* 5th edition, chapters 19 and 26.

Mullins, L.J., *Management and Organisational Behaviour,* 4th edition, chapter 9.

Needham, D. et al., *Business for Higher Awards,* chapters 9, 26, 27 and 28.

Cross-referencing   This element could be cross-referenced to any unit, depending on the nature of the evidence selected.

Element **D4.4**   Advise and inform others

Performance Criterion

(f) *You confirm your recipient's understanding of the information and advice you have given.*

> Detail examples where you have invited confirmatory feedback regarding advice you have given. This may be verbal or written. Explain how you ensured understanding on the part of your recipient.

Interpretation

- How do you confirm understanding?

- Do you actively seek feedback confirming understanding or relevance of the advice and information you have provided?

- Do you tailor your responses based on your knowledge of individual recipients, for example by avoiding jargon?

Candidate illustration

Event route
Kieron continued to focus on the introduction of a new product to the sales force (see PC (b)). Following his presentation, he invited questions from them regarding the information provided. Kieron noted some of these questions as evidence as they clearly demonstrated that the sales force had not understood some of the technical detail. Kieron also obtained witness testimonies from two of the sales force who had asked questions.

Event route
Val was also able to cross-reference to existing evidence. Following the review of the induction process for the new employee (see PC (e)), Val carried out an initial supervision session in line with organisational requirements. The initial session was noted using standard documentation and provided the new employee with an opportunity to clarify issues and ask questions regarding the job, work environment, expectations, requirements, policy and procedures. Val highlighted examples where she had assisted in clarifying points of information and explained the process in a personal statement.

Ideas for evidence

- Notes of questions asked and answers provided.

- Witness testimony from those involved.

- Supervision documentation.

- Correspondence.

Your ideas for evidence

Description of evidence	Location of evidence	Opportunities for cross-referencing	Reflection and analysis

K&U links

Suggested reading for knowledge and understanding purposes:

Cole, G.A., *Management: Theory and Practice,* 5th edition, chapters 19 and 26.

Mullins, L.J., *Management and Organisational Behaviour,* 4th edition, chapter 9.

Needham, D. et al., *Business for Higher Awards,* chapters 9, 26, 27 and 28.

Cross-referencing

This element could be cross-referenced to any unit, depending on the nature of the evidence selected.

Element D4.4   Advise and inform others

Performance Criterion

(g) *You maintain confidentiality according to organisational and legal requirements.*

> We suggest that you focus on specific instances where you have been aware of confidentiality issues when advising and informing others. Detail and evidence your actions in maintaining confidentiality.

Interpretation

■ When advising and informing others, which organisational and legal requirements impact on the information that you provide?

■ How do you ensure that confidentiality is maintained?

Candidate illustration

Event route
Prior to undertaking initial supervision of the new employee (see PC (f)), Val was required to inform him that any discussion would be held as confidential and that only Val and the employee would have access to supervision documentation.

Event route
Kieron cross-referenced to his report to senior management regarding changes in customers' after-sales service requirements (see PC (a)). In the report, Kieron listed the customers that had contributed but, in order to maintain confidentiality, did not identify which customers had made specific comments. The report was highlighted to show the points used as evidence. Kieron also included contractual agreements with customers that confirmed the maintenance of confidentiality over sensitive issues.

Ideas for evidence

■ Details of issues that have required confidentiality.

■ Resources provided to recipients (verbal or written).

■ Contractual obligations.

■ Compliance with organisational requirements.

■ Personal statement.

■ Witness testimony from others involved.

Your ideas for evidence

Description of evidence	Location of evidence	Opportunities for cross-referencing	Reflection and analysis

K&U links

Suggested reading for knowledge and understanding purposes:

Cole, G.A., *Management: Theory and Practice,* 5th edition, chapters 19 and 26.

Mullins, L.J., *Management and Organisational Behaviour,* 4th edition, chapter 9.

Needham, D. et al., *Business for Higher Awards,* chapters 9, 26, 27 and 28.

Cross-referencing

This element could be cross-referenced to any unit, depending on the nature of the evidence selected.

Element D4.4 Advise and inform others

Performance Criterion

(h) *You use feedback from recipients to improve the way you provide advice and information.*

Detail how you obtain and use feedback to confirm or disconfirm your methods of providing information. Use a specific example to demonstrate competence.

Interpretation

▌ Do you actively seek feedback from recipients?

▌ Why is it important to do this?

▌ How do you use feedback?

Candidate illustration

Event route
Callum actively sought feedback on his performance and on the information provided during his assessment of quality assurance monitoring processes (see PC (d)). Feedback was given verbally by various managers. He obtained a testimony to evidence this. He also received written feedback as part of an ongoing assessment of the trainee managers' development programme, which was also submitted. Callum acted on advice and identified the need to be more concise with his reports and actively inform rather than provide background detail. This became part of his personal action plan, which was also submitted as evidence.

Event route
Before finally making an application for funding from the national lottery's grants council (see PC (e)), Rosie took a draft application to personal contacts and internal colleagues in order to obtain feedback prior to making the recommendations to the director. She particularly requested feedback on her written justification part of the application. Responses were written and verbal and correspondence was included as evidence. Rosie illustrated that she used the feedback by including her original draft application and an amended version, highlighting changes and explaining why they were made in a personal statement.

Ideas for evidence

▌ Cross-reference to existing evidence, if appropriate.

▌ Examples of feedback received.

▌ Personal statement explaining circumstances.

▌ Witness testimony from those involved.

▌ Changes made to work as a result of feedback.

Your ideas for evidence

Description of evidence	Location of evidence	Opportunities for cross-referencing	Reflection and analysis

K&U links

Suggested reading for knowledge and understanding purposes:

Cole, G.A., *Management: Theory and Practice,* 5th edition, chapters 19 and 26.

Mullins, L.J., *Management and Organisational Behaviour,* 4th edition, chapter 9.

Needham, D. et al., *Business for Higher Awards,* chapters 9, 26, 27 and 28.

Cross-referencing

This element could be cross-referenced to any unit, depending on the nature of the evidence selected.

Manage the use of physical resources

Element B2.1 Plan the use of physical resources

Performance Criterion

(a) *You give opportunities to relevant people to provide information about the physical resources required.*

> You should focus on specific instances where you have planned for the use of physical resources and have involved relevant people in this planning process. Relevant people should include at least two from the following: team members, colleagues working at the same level, higher-level managers, or sponsors and people outside your organisation. Physical resources can include any of the following: equipment, materials, premises, services and energy.

Interpretation

▊ Under what circumstances have you involved others in identifying physical resources?

▊ Who were they?

▊ What kind of information did you require?

Candidate illustration

Event route
Val was planning a three-day outward-bound team-building event for her team. The need for this arose through supervision sessions with individual members of the team and a general feeling of disparity apparent at team meetings. Val proposed the event at a team meeting and invited feedback about the type of event they wanted (i.e. a service) from team members and her line manager. The feedback, in written, electronic and verbal form, was used as evidence, and Val explained the event in her analysis and through a brief personal statement.

Event route
Callum continued to focus on the preparation for an extra order of drilling products from a major customer (see Unit C2, Element C2.2, PC (g)). His remit was increased to calculate costs and time implications of the additional manufacturing and production of the products. Based on the order of the products, he sought advice from products, purchasing and finance managers, and undertook research into suppliers' costs for the extra equipment and materials needed. Replies from internal personnel and quotes for components from suppliers were submitted as evidence. Callum explained his remit in the analysis of evidence section of his portfolio.

Ideas for evidence

▊ Requests for suggestions as to the kinds of resources required.

▊ Replies from those consulted.

▊ Personal statement detailing the context of the actions taken.

▊ Witness testimony from others involved.

Your ideas for evidence

Description of evidence	Location of evidence	Opportunities for cross-referencing	Reflection and analysis

K&U links

Suggested reading for knowledge and understanding purposes:

Cole, G.A., *Management: Theory and Practice,* 5th edition, chapters 16, 17, pp. 138–41 and chapter 19.

Needham, D. et al., *Business for Higher Awards,* chapters 9 and 17.

Cross-referencing

Evidence and knowledge from this element can be used in the following mandatory units of NVQ Management Level 4: **A2, C2**; and the following optional units: **E5, F6, G1, G2**.

| *Element B2.1* | **Plan the use of physical resources** |

Performance Criterion

(b) *Your plans take account of relevant past experience, trends and developments and factors likely to affect future resource use.*

> Again it is beneficial to focus on a specific instance. Detail all the factors that were relevant to the planning process. Explain significant factors and their effect on your plans for future use of physical resources. Your plans should encompass at least two of the following throughout the element: short term, medium term and long term.

Interpretation

- What kinds of plans have you produced?
- Which factors impacted on the plans?
- What was the nature of the impact?

Candidate illustration

Event route
Val was able to consult with other team members who had arranged similar team-building events to gain an insight into their previous experiences. The conversations were noted and used as evidence. In addition, Val needed to consider workloads, staff coverage for the office, team holidays and client needs. She submitted a personal statement detailing these.

Event route
As a trainee manager, Callum often had to rely on the past experiences of more senior managers. He was able to cross-reference to the evidence used for PC (a), where he had consulted a range of managers regarding the implications of the extra order.

Ideas for evidence

- Details of factors affecting plans.
- Personal statement detailing these.
- Cross-reference to existing evidence, if appropriate.
- Factors concerning time, costs, the resources themselves and the people involved.

Your ideas for evidence

Description of evidence	Location of evidence	Opportunities for cross-referencing	Reflection and analysis

K&U links

Suggested reading for knowledge and understanding purposes:

Cole, G.A., *Management: Theory and Practice,* 5th edition, chapters 16, 17, pp. 138–41 and chapter 19.

Needham, D. et al., *Business for Higher Awards,* chapters 9 and 17.

Cross-referencing

Evidence and knowledge from this element can be used in the following mandatory units of NVQ Management Level 4: **A2, C2**; and the following optional units: **E5, F6, G1, G2**.

Element B2.1 Plan the use of physical resources

Performance Criterion

(c) *Your plans are consistent with your organisation's objectives, policies and legal requirements.*

> You will need to identify and explain the organisational or internal factors that were considered during the planning process. Detail their implications when planning for the use of resources.

Interpretation

▪ Which organisational policies and objectives impacted on resource planning?

▪ Were there legal requirements to take into consideration?

▪ How did you ensure that your plans were congruent with, and supportive of, your organisation's objectives and policies?

Candidate illustration

Event route
Val cleared the idea for the team-building event with her line manager. Her manager was concerned about staff replacement implications and legal requirements concerning clients. Val had to ensure office cover and that the equal opportunities policy was not contravened by expecting team members to attend outside working hours. These were all detailed in Val's information pack about the planned event that was provided to team members.

Event route
Callum used a personal report to detail the legal requirements concerning production methods, materials used and the key objectives, which were profit driven, relevant to his remit. In addition, he obtained advice from production specialists concerning protective clothing and maximum hours of work. This written advice was also used as evidence for this performance criterion.

Ideas for evidence

▪ Examples of organisational objectives, policy and legal requirements, together with how they have been monitored.

▪ Personal report detailing your actions and the organisational context.

▪ Notes obtained from others within, or external to, your organisation.

Your ideas for evidence

Description of evidence	Location of evidence	Opportunities for cross-referencing	Reflection and analysis

K&U links

Suggested reading for knowledge and understanding purposes:

Cole, G.A., *Management: Theory and Practice,* 5th edition, chapters 16, 17, pp. 138–41 and chapter 19.

Needham, D. et al., *Business for Higher Awards,* chapters 9 and 17.

Cross-referencing

Evidence and knowledge from this element can be used in the following mandatory units of NVQ Management Level 4: **A2, C2**; and the following optional units: **E5, F6, G1, G2**.

Element B2.1   Plan the use of physical resources

Performance Criterion

(d) *You present your plans to relevant people in an appropriate and timely manner.*

> To meet the requirements of this PC you will need to explain your chosen methods of presenting your plans. Detail the content and the people involved. People involved should include at least two of the following: team members, peers, higher-level managers, or sponsors and people outside your organisation.

Interpretation

▮ Why were your methods of presenting your plans appropriate?

▮ Did the nature of the plans and knowledge of the people involved impact on your methods of presentation?

▮ What were the timescales involved?

Candidate illustration

Event route

In order to obtain final authority to undertake the team-building event, Val had to produce a briefing account for her manager and the branch manager. This contained justifications for the event, resources needed and likely expenditure, and also detailed how Val intended to resource the event and comply with organisational procedures. The report was annotated and submitted as evidence. The date of the report showed that Val had given the recipients plenty of time to read and digest its contents and make an informed decision, well in advance of the date planned for the event.

Event route

Callum discussed his plans for the production of the extra order with his line manager at his next supervision meeting, as this was an appropriate and timely opportunity. Notes of the supervision and agreed action were included as evidence.

Ideas for evidence

▮ Reports explaining or justifying plans for the use of physical resources.

▮ Notes of discussions.

▮ Guidance derived from presentations that you have given.

▮ An explanation of your method of presentation and timescale involved.

Your ideas for evidence

Description of evidence	Location of evidence	Opportunities for cross-referencing	Reflection and analysis

K&U links

Suggested reading for knowledge and understanding purposes:

Cole, G.A., *Management: Theory and Practice,* 5th edition, chapters 16, 17, pp. 138–41 and chapter 19.

Needham, D. et al., *Business for Higher Awards,* chapters 9 and 17.

Cross-referencing

Evidence and knowledge from this element can be used in the following mandatory units of NVQ Management Level 4: **A2**, **C2**; and the following optional units: **E5**, **F6**, **G1**, **G2**.

Element B2.2 Obtain physical resources

Performance Criterion

(a) *Your requests for physical resources clearly show the costs involved and the anticipated benefits you expect from the use of resources.*

> You will need to detail specific instances where you have requested physical resources. These must be both spoken and written. Explain the organisational context and your actions in justifying the request.

Interpretation

▌ What kinds of resources have you requested?

▌ How were the resources requested?

▌ Was cost–benefit analysis undertaken and included in the request?

Candidate illustration

Event route
To meet the written requirements of this PC, Val was able to cross-reference to the report referenced in Element B2.1, PC (d). Again, she highlighted the relevant sections of the report that justified expenditure and indicated likely costs of subsistence, learning materials for the event, commissioning an external trainer, and booking the premises and equipment to be used.

Event route
Callum detailed his proposals in a briefing document that had to be agreed by his training mentor and line manager before resources could be purchased to begin production for the drilling products order. The briefing document identifying supply costs, worker hours involved and estimated production time was used as evidence, together with a witness testimony from Callum's line manager confirming his actions and also confirming that Callum had made these requests, verbally, during an informal meeting.

Ideas for evidence

▌ Documents and reports justifying expenditure and plans through cost–benefit analysis.

▌ Briefing papers.

▌ Witness testimony from those involved.

Your ideas for evidence

Description of evidence	Location of evidence	Opportunities for cross-referencing	Reflection and analysis

K&U links

Suggested reading for knowledge and understanding purposes:

Cole, G.A., *Management: Theory and Practice,* 5th edition, chapters 19, 28 and 29.

Needham, D. et al., *Business for Higher Awards,* chapters 9 and 17.

Cross-referencing

Evidence and knowledge from this element can be used in the following mandatory units of NVQ Management Level 4: **A2**, **C2**; and the following optional units: **E5**, **F6**, **G1**, **G2**.

Element B2.2   Obtain physical resources

Performance Criterion

(b) You present your requests for physical resources to relevant people in time for the necessary resources to be obtained.

> You should link to PC (a), if appropriate. Explain how requests were presented and who the relevant people were. They must include at least two of the following groups: team members, peers, higher-level managers, or sponsors and people outside your organisation. Detail the timescales involved and their significance.

Interpretation

■ Under what circumstances have you presented requests for physical resources?

■ Who else was involved in the presentation?

■ How did timescales impact on your actions?

Candidate illustration

Event route
Both Val and Callum cross-referenced to the reports used in PC (a). In addition, they included personal statements detailing the people to whom they forwarded their reports and the significance of the timescales involved.

Event route
Callum also included an extract from some of his supervision notes where timescales for the project were agreed with his line manager.

Ideas for evidence

■ Cross-reference to other evidence used for this unit, if appropriate.

■ Examples of requests put forward.

■ Details of people to whom requests were made, in the form of personal statements or witness testimony.

■ Indications of the timescales involved.

Your ideas for evidence

Description of evidence	Location of evidence	Opportunities for cross-referencing	Reflection and analysis

K&U links

Suggested reading for knowledge and understanding purposes:

Cole, G.A., *Management: Theory and Practice*, 5th edition, chapters 19, 28 and 29.

Needham, D. et al., *Business for Higher Awards,* chapters 9 and 17.

Cross-referencing

Evidence and knowledge from this element can be used in the following mandatory units of NVQ Management Level 4: **A2, C2**; and the following optional units: **E5, F6, G1, G2**.

Element B2.2   Obtain physical resources

Performance Criterion

(c) You present requests for physical resources in ways which reflect the commitment of those who will be using the resources.

> Link to previous evidence, if appropriate. Explain how you presented your case for the resources. Detail those who would be using the resources and their input into your request. Illustrate your evidence with specific examples of the impact that obtaining the resources would have on resource users.

Interpretation

- How was the request presented?
- Was the method of presentation influenced by the requirements of resource users?
- What was the organisational context?
- What were the implications of obtaining or not obtaining the physical resources requested?

Candidate illustration

Event route
Val again cross-referenced to the report used in PCs (a) and (b). In it she justified the need for the team-building event and explained the circumstances under which the event had been conceived.

Event route
Callum submitted a personal statement for this performance criterion, explaining the likely overtime that would be made available to workers as a result of the order. In addition, he cross-referenced to Unit C2, Element C2.2, PC (g), where shift patterns were discussed with workers willing to alter work times to accommodate the order. These points were also highlighted in the briefing document submitted for PC (a), which was also cross-referenced as evidence here.

Ideas for evidence

- Cross-reference to existing evidence used in this unit, if appropriate.
- Personal statement explaining actions taken and their implications.
- Extracts from reports detailing the use of resources.
- Witness testimony from others involved.

Your ideas for evidence

Description of evidence	Location of evidence	Opportunities for cross-referencing	Reflection and analysis

K&U links

Suggested reading for knowledge and understanding purposes:

Cole, G.A., *Management: Theory and Practice,* 5th edition, chapters 19, 28 and 29.

Needham, D. et al., *Business for Higher Awards,* chapters 9 and 17.

Cross-referencing

Evidence and knowledge from this element can be used in the following mandatory units of NVQ Management Level 4: **A2, C2**; and the following optional units: **E5, F6, G1, G2**.

Element B2.2 Obtain physical resources

| Performance Criterion | *(d) The physical resources you obtain are sufficient to support all activities within your control.* |

> Again, link to evidence and analysis previously included for this element, if appropriate. Emphasis here is on sufficiency of resources. Detail any calculations you have made in order to identify quantities of specific resources. Justify your calculations, including the nature of the activities for which the resources will be used.

Interpretation

- How do you ensure sufficiency of resources?
- Are calculations made?
- What is the basis of these calculations?

Candidate illustration

Event route
Val consulted with the training section of her department to ensure that she had included all the training materials necessary to run the team-building event. She had neglected to request staff to bring outdoor clothing and also needed to obtain access to some equipment for one of the exercises. Evidence consisted of correspondence with the training section, together with a memo sent to staff listing what they needed to bring with them.

Event route
Callum confirmed the amount of components needed based on calculations made. The original order for the equipment, together with the calculations and a final list of components needed, were submitted as evidence.

Ideas for evidence

- Correspondence confirming amounts of resources required.
- Calculations relating to sufficiency of resources.
- Personal statement explaining actions.

Your ideas for evidence

Description of evidence	Location of evidence	Opportunities for cross-referencing	Reflection and analysis

K&U links

Suggested reading for knowledge and understanding purposes:

Cole, G.A., *Management: Theory and Practice,* 5th edition, chapters 19, 28 and 29.

Needham, D. et al., *Business for Higher Awards,* chapters 9 and 17.

Cross-referencing

Evidence and knowledge from this element can be used in the following mandatory units of NVQ Management Level 4: **A2, C2**; and the following optional units: **E5, F6, G1, G2**.

Element B2.2 Obtain physical resources

Performance Criterion

(e) *Where you cannot obtain the physical resources you need in full, you agree appropriate amendments to your plans with relevant people.*

> Focus on specific instances where plans have been changed in order to accommodate changes in numbers or types of physical resources available. Explain the changes or moderations to your plans and the impact that they will have on your activities. Appropriate people should include at least two of the following: team members, peers, higher-level managers, or sponsors and people outside your organisation.

Interpretation

- In what circumstances have you been unable to obtain the physical resources requested?
- What have been the consequences?
- Who else has been involved?
- How have amendments to plans been agreed?

Candidate illustration

Event route
Val initially wanted her event to be residential and requested quotations for two nights' accommodation at several training centres in the region. The quotes exceeded available funds, so Val revised her plans to ensure that the event was conveniently relocated to enable team members to commute from home. The quotations, together with the final booking for a non-residential course, were used as evidence.

Event route
During his project, Callum received a memo from the production manager regarding production line availability and timing. To avoid disrupting routine production, Callum had scheduled production for the additional order around existing runs. The memo was used as evidence, together with a cross-reference to Unit C2, Element C2.2, PC (g), where Callum had altered shift patterns in consultation with workers to accommodate the extra order.

Ideas for evidence

- Correspondence indicating the need to change plans.
- Evidence forming the basis of changes, quotations, diary extracts, email, correspondence.
- Reports or memos detailing changes.
- Cross-references where appropriate.

Your ideas for evidence

Description of evidence	Location of evidence	Opportunities for cross-referencing	Reflection and analysis

K&U links

Suggested reading for knowledge and understanding purposes:

Cole, G.A., *Management: Theory and Practice,* 5th edition, chapters 19, 28 and 29.

Needham, D. et al., *Business for Higher Awards,* chapters 9 and 17.

Cross-referencing

Evidence and knowledge from this element can be used in the following mandatory units of NVQ Management Level 4: **A2**, **C2**; and the following optional units: **E5**, **F6**, **G1**, **G2**.

Element B2.3 **Ensure availability of supplies**

Performance Criterion

(a) You identify the supplies you need accurately.

> In this context, supplies are defined as the ongoing provision of goods and services required. Detail the nature of the supplies you need. Explain any calculations or research to ensure that you accurately identify the correct supplies.

Interpretation

■ What supplies are needed to ensure that the provision of goods or services is maintained to the required level?

■ How do you ensure that the supplies are suitable?

Candidate illustration

Event route
Rosie focused on the supplies needed to maintain fundraising activities on behalf of her charity. These included communications systems, pagers and mobile phones, volunteers with their own vehicles, venues to run events, sponsorship from companies, and rewards to encourage people to undertake fundraising events. Rosie illustrated competence for this element by taking the event route and detailing a major project, which was to arrange a sponsored cycle across the island of Sicily. Rosie initially compiled a briefing document for the charity board detailing proposals and resources needed, and explaining how costs would be met. She highlighted the resource section as evidence here.

Event route
Callum continued to focus on his project concerning the additional order of drilling products from a major distributor (see Unit C2, Element C2.2, PC (g)). He was able to cross-reference to evidence used in this unit, detailing the components needed to manufacture the order.

Ideas for evidence

■ Cross-reference to existing evidence, if appropriate.

■ Details of any supplies needed and how they are identified.

■ Explanation of the calculations made in identifying the resources.

Your ideas for evidence

Description of evidence	Location of evidence	Opportunities for cross-referencing	Reflection and analysis

K&U links

Suggested reading for knowledge and understanding purposes:

Cole, G.A., *Management: Theory and Practice,* 5th edition, chapters 19, 28 and 29.

Needham, D. et al., *Business for Higher Awards,* chapters 9 and 17.

Cross-referencing

Evidence and knowledge from this element can be used in the following mandatory units of NVQ Management Level 4: **A2, C2**; and the following optional units: **E5, F6, G1, G2**.

Element B2.3   **Ensure availability of supplies**

Performance Criterion	*(b) The range of suppliers from which you choose is sufficiently wide to ensure adequate competition and continuity of suppliers.*

> Explain who your suppliers are. Detail the basis on which suppliers are used and the nature of organisational agreements with suppliers. Suppliers should include those inside and outside your organisation.

Interpretation

- Who are the suppliers relevant to your area of responsibility?
- On what basis are they contracted or commissioned?
- How do you ensure continuity of supply?

Candidate illustration

Event route
In costing the project detailed in PC (a) of this element, Rosie contacted several suppliers of air travel, accommodation, cycle equipment, first aid supplies, printing and stationery. Details of her quotations were used as evidence of choosing supplies from a range of suppliers.

Event route
Callum's company drew from a wide range of suppliers. Callum obtained quotations from each and asked for component specifications, which were evidenced here. In addition, Callum included a witness testimony from his line manager confirming that he was aware of company policy expecting suppliers to provide components to the right specification, in the correct quantity and within agreed timescales.

Ideas for evidence

- Evidence detailing different suppliers.
- Criteria for the contracting of suppliers.
- Personal statement explaining organisational context of evidence.
- Witness testimony confirming your actions or approach.

Your ideas for evidence

Description of evidence	Location of evidence	Opportunities for cross-referencing	Reflection and analysis

K&U links

Suggested reading for knowledge and understanding purposes:

Cole, G.A., *Management: Theory and Practice,* 5th edition, chapters 19, 28 and 29.

Needham, D. et al., *Business for Higher Awards,* chapters 9 and 17.

Cross-referencing

Evidence and knowledge from this element can be used in the following mandatory units of NVQ Management Level 4: **A2, C2**; and the following optional units: **E5, F6, G1, G2**.

Element B2.3 Ensure availability of supplies

Performance Criterion	(c) *You negotiate with suppliers in a manner which will maintain good relations with them.*

> You should highlight specific instances where you have had contact with suppliers. Detail the context of any negotiations and the outcome.

Interpretation

▮ In what circumstances have you negotiated with internal or external suppliers?

▮ What was the nature of negotiations?

▮ Which skills did you use to maintain positive relationships with suppliers?

Candidate illustration

Event route
Rosie submitted two examples of correspondence with travel and cycle equipment suppliers. She was trying to obtain discounts as the charity was making block bookings and orders. She also offered free publicity to the companies in return for discounts.

Event route
Callum submitted notes of conversations held with suppliers concerning delivery dates for components. In addition, he obtained a testimony from his line manager confirming his negotiating skills.

Ideas for evidence

▮ Correspondence with suppliers.

▮ Notes of conversations with suppliers.

▮ Examples of the outcomes of negotiations.

▮ Witness testimony confirming your actions.

Your ideas for evidence

Description of evidence	Location of evidence	Opportunities for cross-referencing	Reflection and analysis

K&U links

Suggested reading for knowledge and understanding purposes:

Cole, G.A., *Management: Theory and Practice*, 5th edition, chapters 19, 28 and 29.

Needham, D. et al., *Business for Higher Awards*, chapters 9 and 17.

Cross-referencing

Evidence and knowledge from this element can be used in the following mandatory units of NVQ Management Level 4: **A2**, **C2**; and the following optional units: **E5**, **F6**, **G1**, **G2**.

Element B2.3 Ensure availability of supplies

Performance Criterion

(d) The agreements you reach with suppliers provide good value and comply with organisational and legal requirements.

> Link to previous evidence for this element, if appropriate. Explain the nature of agreements. You may be able to show comparisons with other suppliers to illustrate value. Detail any organisational or legal requirements that impact on the nature of supplies or on the agreements that you reach with suppliers.

Interpretation

▎ What kinds of agreement do you have with suppliers?

▎ How do you ensure that they provide good value?

▎ How do you or your organisation define good value?

▎ Which organisational and legal requirements impact on suppliers' agreements?

Candidate illustration

Event route
Rosie detailed negotiations with air travel suppliers (see PC (c) of this element). She obtained a reduced block booking for 40 people to fly to Sicily, in return for which the airline would receive free advertising opportunities throughout the project. This was confirmed through correspondence and agreed by the charity board. Minutes of the meeting with the charity board were also included. Rosie also cross-referenced to the briefing document submitted for PC (a) of this element.

Event route
Callum was able to cross-reference to the evidence submitted for PCs (b) and (c), which detailed agreements and confirmed his compliance with organisational requirements.

Ideas for evidence

▎ Cross-reference to existing evidence, if appropriate.

▎ Final agreements or contracts with suppliers.

▎ Detail of organisational or legal requirements.

Your ideas for evidence

Description of evidence	Location of evidence	Opportunities for cross-referencing	Reflection and analysis

K&U links

Suggested reading for knowledge and understanding purposes:

Cole, G.A., *Management: Theory and Practice*, 5th edition, chapters 19, 28 and 29.

Needham, D. et al., *Business for Higher Awards*, chapters 9 and 17.

Cross-referencing

Evidence and knowledge from this element can be used in the following mandatory units of NVQ Management Level 4: **A2**, **C2**; and the following optional units: **E5**, **F6**, **G1**, **G2**.

Element B2.3 Ensure availability of supplies

Performance Criterion

(e) *You monitor the quality and quantity of supplies at appropriate intervals.*

> Focus on specific instances where you have performed checks on supplies, or managed the process. Explain any systems that can be used for this purpose and your involvement. Detail the timescales involved and explain why these are appropriate.

Interpretation

▌ How do you ensure that the quantity and quality of supplies are appropriate?

▌ What kinds of systems are employed?

What responsibility do you have for this process?

Candidate illustration

Event route
Rosie focused on the supply of medical and first aid equipment for the sponsored event. Through consultation with a health and safety medical expert, she ensured that the supplies identified were appropriate and sufficient for the ten-day trip. Correspondence was submitted as evidence. On delivery of the supplies, Rosie checked that the delivery note complied with the original order. Both of these documents, signed by Rosie, were also submitted as evidence.

Event route
While spending time in the production department as part of his training programme, Callum oversaw the quality control procedure relating to goods inward. He used the relevant documentation as evidence here.

Ideas for evidence

▌ Cross-reference to existing evidence used in the NVQ, if appropriate.

▌ Evidence of monitoring: documentation and paperwork.

▌ Confirmation of quantity of orders using delivery notes and receipts.

Your ideas for evidence

Description of evidence	Location of evidence	Opportunities for cross-referencing	Reflection and analysis

K&U links

Suggested reading for knowledge and understanding purposes:

Cole, G.A., *Management: Theory and Practice*, 5th edition, chapters 19, 28 and 29.

Needham, D. et al., *Business for Higher Awards*, chapters 9 and 17.

Cross-referencing

Evidence and knowledge from this element can be used in the following mandatory units of NVQ Management Level 4: **A2, C2**; and the following optional units: **E5, F6, G1, G2**.

Element B2.3 **Ensure availability of supplies**

Performance Criterion

(f) The supplies you obtain consistently meet your organisation's requirements for quality, quantity and delivery.

> Again, cross-reference to existing evidence used for this unit, where appropriate. Focus on the nature of the supplies and the alternatives that you choose not to use. Explain any organisational requirements and how you ensure that they are met.

Interpretation

▪ Cross-reference to existing evidence, if appropriate.

▪ How do you ensure consistency of supplies?

▪ What organisational requirements impact upon levels of quality and quantity and delivery of supplies?

Candidate illustration

Event route
Rosie cross-referenced to evidence used throughout this unit in the form of the briefing document. She highlighted examples of the supplies obtained and included the feedback from the charity board accepting the project.

Event route
Callum cross-referenced to evidence used in PC (b) of this element, detailing company requirements. He also submitted correspondence with suppliers accepting proposals and final contracts detailing the quantity and delivery dates of the components.

Ideas for evidence

▪ Cross-reference to existing evidence, if appropriate.

▪ Details of supplies obtained.

▪ Agreements and contracts made with suppliers.

▪ Examples of compliance with organisational policy, procedures and requirements.

Your ideas for evidence

Description of evidence	Location of evidence	Opportunities for cross-referencing	Reflection and analysis

K&U links

Suggested reading for knowledge and understanding purposes:

Cole, G.A., *Management: Theory and Practice*, 5th edition, chapters 19, 28 and 29.

Needham, D. et al., *Business for Higher Awards*, chapters 9 and 17.

Cross-referencing

Evidence and knowledge from this element can be used in the following mandatory units of NVQ Management Level 4: **A2**, **C2**; and the following optional units: **E5**, **F6**, **G1**, **G2**.

| *Element* B2.3 | **Ensure availability of supplies** |

Performance Criterion

(g) *You deal with any actual or potential problems with supplies promptly.*

> Focus on specific problems that you have experienced. Explain the circumstances and the actions taken in dealing with these problems.

Interpretation

■ Under what circumstances have you had to deal with problems with supplies?

■ What action was taken?

■ What were the timescales involved and how were they significant?

Candidate illustration

Event route
Rosie had to deal with potential problems concerning flying times. All the volunteers involved in the sponsored cycle would have to travel at the same time. However, accommodation on Sicily had not yet been arranged. Rosie contacted the airline and requested flexibility of flying dates for a predetermined time, giving herself space to arrange accommodation and then confirm with the airline. Notes of conversations and faxes sent and returned were included as evidence.

Event route
Callum continued to focus on the additional order for which he had been given responsibility. A problem occurred when the supplier of a particular component could not deliver the quantity needed to complete the job. Callum contacted an alternative supplier to obtain the component in time so as to avoid delays in production. He included correspondence with the original and alternative suppliers as evidence.

Ideas for evidence

■ Details of correspondence with suppliers concerning problems:
  – emails;
  – faxes;
  – letters.

■ Personal statement explaining context and impact of problems and the actions taken.

Your ideas for evidence

Description of evidence	Location of evidence	Opportunities for cross-referencing	Reflection and analysis

K&U links

Suggested reading for knowledge and understanding purposes:

Cole, G.A., *Management: Theory and Practice*, 5th edition, chapters 19, 28 and 29.

Needham, D. et al., *Business for Higher Awards*, chapters 9 and 17.

Cross-referencing

Evidence and knowledge from this element can be used in the following mandatory units of NVQ Management Level 4: **A2**, **C2**; and the following optional units: **E5**, **F6**, **G1**, **G2**.

Element B2.3   Ensure availability of supplies

Performance Criterion

(h) Your records of supplies are complete, accurate and available only to authorised people.

> Explain your invoice, delivery, storage and requisition record systems. Detail how these records are maintained in line with confidentiality requirements.

Interpretation

- What kinds of records are kept?
- What is your role in ensuring that records are completed and are accurate?
- How is access restricted?

Candidate illustration

Event route
Rosie and Callum simply cross-referenced to examples of documentation already used as evidence for this element.

Callum also detailed the storage and retrieval system in operation in a personal statement confirming restriction of access to this information.

Ideas for evidence

- Examples of complete and accurate records.
- Details of measures taken to ensure confidentiality is maintained:
  - computer passwords;
  - ID badges;
  - storage and retrieval systems.

Your ideas for evidence

Description of evidence	Location of evidence	Opportunities for cross-referencing	Reflection and analysis

K&U links

Suggested reading for knowledge and understanding purposes:

Cole, G.A., *Management: Theory and Practice*, 5th edition, chapters 19, 28 and 29.

Needham, D. et al., *Business for Higher Awards*, chapters 9 and 17.

Cross-referencing

Evidence and knowledge from this element can be used in the following mandatory units of NVQ Management Level 4: **A2, C2**; and the following optional units: **E5, F6, G1, G2**.

Element B2.4 Monitor the use of physical resources

Performance Criterion

(a) *You give opportunities to team members to take individual responsibility for the efficient use of physical resources.*

> You should explain specific instances where you have provided these kinds of opportunities. Don't forget to detail the circumstances and how team members ensured the efficient use of resources.

Interpretation

■ How have you provided these kinds of opportunities?

■ Who were the team members involved?

■ What were the circumstances?

■ How did your actions improve the efficient use of resources?

Candidate illustration

Event route
Rosie continued with her account of the sponsored cycle project (see Element B2.3). Once the allocation of resources was agreed, Rosie delegated responsibility for specific areas of the project to members of her team. This included distributing promotional material to attract volunteers and monitoring the use of cycling equipment, provisions and medical supplies. Rosie gave each member of her team a specific remit. This information was included as evidence.

Event route
Callum also continued to focus on the production of the special order of drilling products. Production workers routinely recorded components used and detailed any faulty or incomplete supplies. These were monitored using standardised documentation and checked daily by the supervisor, in this case Callum. Several of the records were submitted as evidence, together with a personal statement from Callum explaining the process.

Ideas for evidence

■ Details in writing of delegated responsibility to team members:
   – supervision notes;
   – written notes.

■ Witness testimonies from team members.

Your ideas for evidence

Description of evidence	Location of evidence	Opportunities for cross-referencing	Reflection and analysis

K&U links Suggested reading for knowledge and understanding purposes:

Cole, G.A., *Management: Theory and Practice,* 5th edition, chapters 19, 28 and 29.

Needham, D. et al., *Business for Higher Awards,* chapters 9 and 17.

Cross-referencing Evidence and knowledge from this element can be used in the following mandatory units of NVQ Management Level 4: **A2, C2**; and the following optional units: **E5, F6, G1, G2**.

Element B2.4 Monitor the use of physical resources

Performance Criterion

(b) Your team's use of physical resources is efficient and takes into account the possible impact on the environment.

> Link to PC (a) of this element, if appropriate. Detail how you ensure that resources are used efficiently. Explain any measures that are taken to ensure that, where possible, the use of resources is environmentally friendly.

Interpretation

■ What kinds of resources are used by your team in order to provide products or services?

■ How is efficiency monitored?

■ What environmental considerations impact on the use of these resources?

Candidate illustration

Event route
Rosie focused on the use of stationery and the recycling policy operated by her organisation. She included the policy statement and detailed in a personal statement how waste paper was used for scrap and how envelopes were recycled, where possible.

Event route
Callum focused on the use of packaging that came from the supplies used in production. He obtained a witness testimony from his line manager detailing the processes used in recycling packaging. Callum also included the documentation used when components were found to be faulty and returned to the suppliers. He explained the process in his analysis, detailing the monitoring and return of faulty components to ensure efficiency in terms of usage, costs and time.

Ideas for evidence

■ Evidence of compliance with organisational requirements regarding environmental issues.

■ Personal statement detailing actions taken.

■ Documentation used to monitor efficiency.

■ Witness testimony from others involved.

Your ideas for evidence

Description of evidence	Location of evidence	Opportunities for cross-referencing	Reflection and analysis

K&U links

Suggested reading for knowledge and understanding purposes:

Cole, G.A., *Management: Theory and Practice,* 5th edition, chapters 19, 28 and 29.

Needham, D. et al., *Business for Higher Awards,* chapters 9 and 17.

Cross-referencing

Evidence and knowledge from this element can be used in the following mandatory units of NVQ Management Level 4: **A2, C2**; and the following optional units: **E5, F6, G1, G2**.

Element **B2.4**   **Monitor the use of physical resources**

Performance Criterion

(c)   You monitor the quality of physical resources continuously.

> Cross-reference to other evidence used in this unit, if appropriate. Explain the nature of the physical resource for which you are responsible and how quality is monitored. Use specific examples to illustrate competence.

Interpretation

- Does the nature of the physical resources for which you are responsible define how quality is monitored?
- How is this undertaken continuously?
- Why is it important to monitor quality?

Candidate illustration

Event route
Throughout the sponsored cycle project, Rosie monitored the delivery of materials and services against agreed specifications. Documentation relating to delivery and inspections undertaken was included as evidence.

Event route
Callum also continuously monitored the quality of components used in the production of the drilling equipment. This was done on delivery and throughout the production process, and documentation was completed accordingly. Examples of monitoring documentation were submitted, together with a witness testimony from Callum's line manager confirming his actions.

Ideas for evidence

- Quality monitoring documentation.
- Personal statement detailing methods of monitoring quality.
- Witness testimony from others involved.
- Outcomes of monitoring.

Your ideas for evidence

Description of evidence	Location of evidence	Opportunities for cross-referencing	Reflection and analysis

K&U links   Suggested reading for knowledge and understanding purposes:

Cole, G.A., *Management: Theory and Practice*, 5th edition, chapters 19, 28 and 29.

Needham, D. et al., *Business for Higher Awards*, chapters 9 and 17.

Cross-referencing   Evidence and knowledge from this element can be used in the following mandatory units of NVQ Management Level 4: **A2**, **C2**; and the following optional units: **E5**, **F6**, **G1**, **G2**.

Monitor the use of physical resources

Performance Criterion

(d) *Your methods of monitoring the use of physical resources are reliable and comply with organisational requirements.*

> Link to PC (d), if appropriate. Focus on specific methods and explain why they are appropriate. You must show evidence that you use two of the following types of monitoring: your own observation, considering oral information from others, and considering written information from others. Detail any organisational requirements that impact on methods of monitoring physical resources.

Interpretation

▪ Which methods of monitoring do you use?

▪ How do you ensure that they are reliable?

▪ Which organisational requirements do you have to comply with?

Candidate illustration

Event route
Having delegated responsibility to team members, Rosie received a memo from one member of her team suggesting that, to ensure sufficiency of medical supplies, a supplier should be contacted in Sicily in case extra were needed. Rosie agreed the proposal and produced documentation to monitor usage so that trigger points could be identified, indicating the need for further supplies. The memo, together with Rosie's reply and the monitoring documentation, were submitted as evidence.

Event route
Callum was able to cross-reference to Element B2.3, PC (e), where he had evidenced methods of monitoring physical resources during production. Callum illustrated the process in his analysis of evidence.

Ideas for evidence

▪ Cross-reference to existing evidence, if appropriate.

▪ Documentation relating to monitoring of resource usage.

▪ Information received concerning monitoring of resource usage.

▪ Details of actions taken in line with organisational requirements.

Your ideas for evidence

Description of evidence	Location of evidence	Opportunities for cross-referencing	Reflection and analysis

K&U links

Suggested reading for knowledge and understanding purposes:

Cole, G.A., *Management: Theory and Practice,* 5th edition, chapters 19, 28 and 29.

Needham, D. et al., *Business for Higher Awards,* chapters 9 and 17.

Cross-referencing

Evidence and knowledge from this element can be used in the following mandatory units of NVQ Management Level 4: **A2, C2**; and the following optional units: **E5, F6, G1, G2**.

Element B2.4   **Monitor the use of physical resources**

Performance Criterion

(e) *You monitor the actual use of physical resources against an agreed plan at appropriate intervals.*

> Link to previous evidence used in this element, if appropriate, and consider PC (f) before undertaking this one. Focus on how you monitor the use of resources to ensure efficiency against plans. Explain the significance of the timescales involved.

Interpretation

■   How is the efficient use of physical resources monitored?

■   What is your involvement in the monitoring process?

■   What are the timescales involved?

Candidate illustration

Event route
Rosie was able to cross-reference to PC (d) of this element, where she scheduled usage of medical supplies and identified trigger points for additional supplies.

Event route
Callum was also able to cross-reference to Unit D4, Element D4.2, PC (f), where he had implemented a quality assurance system for use of materials on the production line. The evidence was supplemented with a personal statement detailing the methods of monitoring employed, the timescales involved and their significance.

Ideas for evidence

■   Cross-reference to existing evidence, if appropriate.

■   Outcomes of monitoring:
   – completed documentation;
   – computer printouts.

Your ideas for evidence

Description of evidence	Location of evidence	Opportunities for cross-referencing	Reflection and analysis

K&U links

Suggested reading for knowledge and understanding purposes:

Cole, G.A., *Management: Theory and Practice,* 5th edition, chapters 19, 28 and 29.

Needham, D. et al., *Business for Higher Awards,* chapters 9 and 17.

Cross-referencing

Evidence and knowledge from this element can be used in the following mandatory units of NVQ Management Level 4: **A2**, **C2**; and the following optional units: **E5**, **F6**, **G1**, **G2**.

| *Element* B2.4 | Monitor the use of physical resources |

Performance Criterion

(f) *You take prompt corrective action to deal with actual or potential deviations from your plan.*

> You can link to the previous PC, if appropriate. Detail specific instances where actual or potential deviations have occurred. Explain the actions taken in dealing with this. The corrective action taken should include at least two of the following: altering activities, modifying the use of physical resources for activities, and renegotiating the allocation of physical resources.

Interpretation

▌ Under what circumstances has monitoring the use of physical resources identified a potential or actual deviation from your plans?

▌ What action was taken?

▌ What was the outcome?

Candidate illustration

Event route
Rosie was concerned that despite the promotional materials used, response to the cycling event was limited. She therefore contacted a national newspaper to request additional sponsorship in the form of free advertising space. In this way, the charity was able to obtain a front page advert, which attracted many more volunteers.

Event route
While monitoring the materials supplied by one particular manufacturer, Callum found that too many were faulty. He therefore returned the entire delivery to the supplier, requesting a credit note, and contacted an alternative supplier. Details of the returned delivery and the fax sent to an alternative supplier were submitted as evidence, and Callum detailed the situation in his analysis of evidence.

Ideas for evidence

▌ Evidence relating to corrective action taken:
  – returns;
  – correspondence with internal and external people;
  – outcomes of actions taken.

Your ideas for evidence

Description of evidence	Location of evidence	Opportunities for cross-referencing	Reflection and analysis

K&U links

Suggested reading for knowledge and understanding purposes:

Cole, G.A., *Management: Theory and Practice,* 5th edition, chapters 19, 28 and 29.

Needham, D. et al., *Business for Higher Awards,* chapters 9 and 17.

Cross-referencing

Evidence and knowledge from this element can be used in the following mandatory units of NVQ Management Level 4: **A2**, **C2**; and the following optional units: **E5**, **F6**, **G1**, **G2**.

Element B2.4   Monitor the use of physical resources

Performance Criterion	(g) *Your records relating to the use of physical resources are complete, accurate and available to authorised people only.*

> You can link to evidence submitted for previous performance criteria, if appropriate. Explain your records system and detail measures taken that ensure confidentiality.

Interpretation

- What kinds of records are kept concerning the use of physical resources?
- How are they maintained and what role do you play?
- How is confidentiality ensured?

Candidate illustration

Event route
Both Rosie and Callum were able to cross-reference to existing records produced as evidence throughout this element.

Ideas for evidence

- Examples of documentation used and records kept.
- Details of storage and retrieval systems and authorisation levels.

Your ideas for evidence

Description of evidence	Location of evidence	Opportunities for cross-referencing	Reflection and analysis

K&U links

Suggested reading for knowledge and understanding purposes:

Cole, G.A., *Management: Theory and Practice*, 5th edition, chapters 19, 28 and 29.

Needham, D. et al., *Business for Higher Awards*, chapters 9 and 17.

Cross-referencing

Evidence and knowledge from this element can be used in the following mandatory units of NVQ Management Level 4: **A2**, **C2**; and the following optional units: **E5**, **F6**, **G1**, **G2**.

Manage the use of financial resources

Make recommendations for expenditure

Performance Criterion

(a) *You give opportunities to relevant people to make suggestions for future expenditure.*

> You will have to explain your role in assisting others to identify areas for expenditure. Relevant people should include at least two of the following: staff, peers, senior managers and financial specialists. Detail how you provide opportunities, giving evidence of your methods.

Interpretation

▪ Why is it important to involve others in making recommendations for expenditure?

▪ Is this a routine or non-routine occurrence in your job role?

▪ What part do you play in involving others in the process?

Candidate illustration

Event route
Val focused on a routine procedure involving budgeting for her team's expenditure in the coming financial year. Prior to reviewing the previous year's expenditure, she distributed a standardised form to each team member requesting projections of expenditure under specific headings. She then called a meeting to discuss and compare projections, and invited her manager to attend. Examples of the completed budget form, together with minutes of the meeting, were used as evidence.

Event route
Kieron chose to focus this element on the financial implications of his organisation's expansion into European markets. He had identified general budget headings for likely expenditure but needed advice from those with exporting experience. He requested information from the local Business Link office (i.e. financial specialists in this area) and discussed additional budget headings with them. The headings provided by those involved, supported by a witness testimony, were used as evidence.

Ideas for evidence

▪ Minutes of team meetings.

▪ Results of requests for suggestions.

▪ Correspondence requesting input regarding expenditure.

▪ Details of the kinds of expenditure discussed.

Your ideas for evidence

Description of evidence	Location of evidence	Opportunities for cross-referencing	Reflection and analysis

K&U links

Suggested reading for knowledge and understanding purposes:

Cole, G.A., *Management: Theory and Practice,* 5th edition, chapters 19 and 52.

Mullins, L.J., *Management and Organisational Behaviour,* 4th edition, chapter 17.

Needham, D. et al., *Business for Higher Awards,* chapters 8, 16, 17 and 18.

Cross-referencing

Evidence and knowledge from this element can be used in the following mandatory units of NVQ Management Level 4: **A2**, **A4**, **C2**, **D4**; and the following optional units: **C13**, **E3**, **E5**, **E8**.

Element B3.1 Make recommendations for expenditure

Performance Criterion

(b) *Your recommendations take account of past experience, trends, developments and other factors likely to affect future expenditure.*

> Your reflection and analysis should detail how you review previous projected and actual expenditure and use analytical techniques to identify patterns or trends. Explain how you have used this information to ensure that current recommendations are accurate and realistic.

Interpretation

▌ What actions do you take to ensure that previous experiences and occurrences are considered when making recommendations for expenditure?

▌ What kinds of trends and developments have you identified?

▌ How have they impacted on your recommendations?

Candidate illustration

Event route
Following the collection of recommendations from her team, Val compared areas of expenditure and projected expenditure with those of previous years. She identified trends in increased expenditure for several areas over this period, which were explained by increases in resource and material costs and the privatisation of several county services. These increases and an explanation formed part of the appendixes to her budget report, which formed the main body of evidence for this element. The appendixes were labelled and highlighted for ease of assessment.

Event route
During his work on export strategies and market entry into Europe, Kieron consulted with colleagues in other organisations and took advantage of export conferences to network with experienced international sales people. Kieron specifically sought information on national trends in export costs, changes in legislation and European Union directives on exporting. Kieron explained in a personal statement that, as this was a new venture for his organisation, no internal information was available. In his strategic plan for market entry he presented examples of national and European trends and developments that he had analysed. This information was further augmented in the recommendations section. Relevant parts of the report were annotated and highlighted in support of this PC's requirements.

Ideas for evidence

▪ Extracts from relevant reports.

▪ Examples of trends, factors and developments identified.

▪ Personal statement explaining the impact of these trends and developments on future recommendations for expenditure.

▪ Testimony from others involved.

Your ideas for evidence

Description of evidence	Location of evidence	Opportunities for cross-referencing	Reflection and analysis

K&U links

Suggested reading for knowledge and understanding purposes:

Cole, G.A., *Management: Theory and Practice,* 5th edition, chapters 19 and 52.

Mullins, L.J., *Management and Organisational Behaviour,* 4th edition, chapter 17.

Needham, D. et al., *Business for Higher Awards,* chapters 8, 16, 17 and 18.

Cross-referencing

Evidence and knowledge from this element can be used in the following mandatory units of NVQ Management Level 4: **A2, A4, C2, D4**; and the following optional units: **C13, E3, E5, E8**.

Element B3.1   Make recommendations for expenditure

Performance Criterion

(c) *You clearly state the expected benefits from the recommended expenditure, and any potential negative consequences.*

> You will have to detail how you have qualified and justified your recommendations. This may involve cost–benefit analysis and consideration of opportunity cost. Clearly, in providing a balanced recommendation, you must indicate undesirable consequences, their likely impact and how you plan to avoid them.

Interpretation

■ What are the expected benefits of the recommended expenditure?

■ Where and how are they stated?

■ How are they justified and accurate?

■ What are the possible negative consequences?

■ Why is it important to include these in your recommendations?

Candidate illustration

Event route
Val's budget report was designed to support her bid for specific amounts from the central budget. She highlighted the sections justifying the need for continued or, in some cases, increased expenditure in several areas. Benefits were identified as monitoring and improving services to the public and to ensure compliance with changes in legislation. Negative consequences were identified as the increased expenditure needed to do this.

Event route
Kieron justified his recommendations for investment in export materials with projected sales and profit figures. Negative consequences focused on the impact exporting may have on the firm's ability to satisfy the national market.

Ideas for evidence

■ Extracts from relevant reports recommending or justifying expenditure.

■ Explicit examples of benefits and negative consequences.

■ Examples of working notes and calculations.

Your ideas for evidence

Description of evidence	Location of evidence	Opportunities for cross-referencing	Reflection and analysis

K&U links

Suggested reading for knowledge and understanding purposes:

Cole, G.A., *Management: Theory and Practice,* 5th edition, chapters 19 and 52.

Mullins, L.J., *Management and Organisational Behaviour,* 4th edition, chapter 17.

Needham, D. et al., *Business for Higher Awards,* chapters 8, 16, 17 and 18.

Cross-referencing

Evidence and knowledge from this element can be used in the following mandatory units of NVQ Management Level 4: **A2, A4, C2, D4**; and the following optional units: **C13, E3, E5, E8**.

Element B3.1 Make recommendations for expenditure

Performance Criterion

(d) Where you have considered alternative options for expenditure, you provide valid reasons why you have rejected them.

> To meet the requirements of this PC you will have to include examples of alternative options that you have considered. These should include both of the following: other courses of action to achieve the same results and alternative ways of funding the same course.

Interpretation

■ When were alternatives considered?

■ What was their impact?

■ Why were they rejected?

Candidate illustration

Event route
With reference to PCs (a)–(c), Val detailed alternative courses of action in her report. She identified that the majority of these did not support the department's plan for the coming year. Further alternatives would not meet the increasing and changing needs of clients as they merely maintained services at the current level. As an employee of a local government organisation, Val included a personal statement explaining the allocation of finance and options for joint funding with other agencies.

Event route
In his strategy report Kieron explored alternative forms of European market entry, such as foreign direct investment and licensing. These alternatives were rejected because of higher entry costs for the company, but were identified as potential means of expansion in the future. Again, Kieron highlighted the relevant part of his report to the director as evidence.

Ideas for evidence

■ Extracts from relevant reports.

■ Personal statement detailing the context and likely impact of alternative options.

■ Testimony from those involved.

■ Details of presentations given.

■ Notes of discussions concerning options.

■ Minutes of meetings reviewing options.

■ Correspondence concerning options.

Your ideas for evidence

Description of evidence	Location of evidence	Opportunities for cross-referencing	Reflection and analysis

K&U links

Suggested reading for knowledge and understanding purposes:

Cole, G.A., *Management: Theory and Practice*, 5th edition, chapters 19 and 52.

Mullins, L.J., *Management and Organisational Behaviour*, 4th edition, chapter 17.

Needham, D. et al., *Business for Higher Awards*, chapters 8, 16, 17 and 18.

Cross-referencing

Evidence and knowledge from this element can be used in the following mandatory units of NVQ Management Level 4: **A2**, **A4**, **C2**, **D4**; and the following optional units: **C13**, **E3**, **E5**, **E8**.

Element B3.1   Make recommendations for expenditure

Performance Criterion

(e) *You provide sufficient, valid information for relevant people to make decisions on your recommendations.*

You need to highlight the range of information provided to decision takers. Detail reports, explain the nature of presentations and any other qualitative and quantitative information provided.

Interpretation

▌ How do you ensure that the information provided is relevant and sufficient for decision making?

▌ Who are the relevant people?

Candidate illustration

Event route
Both Val and Kieron continued to reference their reports to meet the requirements of this performance criterion.

Kieron was asked by his senior management team to provide additional information concerning projected sales and his calculations. His response was also included as evidence.

Ideas for evidence

▌ Cross-reference to evidence used for this element, if relevant.

▌ Requests for information and your reply.

▌ Requests for additional information and your replies.

Your ideas for evidence

Description of evidence	Location of evidence	Opportunities for cross-referencing	Reflection and analysis

K&U links

Suggested reading for knowledge and understanding purposes:

Cole, G.A., *Management: Theory and Practice*, 5th edition, chapters 19 and 52.

Mullins, L.J., *Management and Organisational Behaviour*, 4th edition, chapter 17.

Needham, D. et al., *Business for Higher Awards*, chapters 8, 16, 17 and 18.

Cross-referencing

Evidence and knowledge from this element can be used in the following mandatory units of NVQ Management Level 4: **A2, A4, C2, D4**; and the following optional units: **C13, E3, E5, E8**.

Element B3.1 Make recommendations for expenditure

Performance Criterion

(f) *Your recommendations for expenditure are consistent with your organisation's plans and objectives.*

Explain how your recommendations support or complement your organisation's plans and objectives. Detail how you have taken plans and objectives into account.

Interpretation

▌ What are the relevant organisational plans and objectives?

▌ How do you ensure that your recommendations for expenditure comply with these?

▌ Do you use plans and objectives in support of your recommendations?

Candidate illustration

Event route
Val's work on budgeting for the coming year sought to meet the aims and objectives of the social services department in terms of providing flexible and client-centred services. This was used as one of the main justifications in her report.

Event route
Kieron was given a specific remit by the director of his organisation to research and provide information on market entry strategies in Europe. He included the written request and referred to his report as evidence.

Ideas for evidence

▌ Extracts from reports showing how recommendations support organisational plans and objectives.

▌ Witness testimony from those involved.

▌ Personal statement explaining circumstances.

Your ideas for evidence

Description of evidence	Location of evidence	Opportunities for cross-referencing	Reflection and analysis

K&U links

Suggested reading for knowledge and understanding purposes:

Cole, G.A., *Management: Theory and Practice*, 5th edition, chapters 19 and 52.

Mullins, L.J., *Management and Organisational Behaviour*, 4th edition, chapter 17.

Needham, D. et al., *Business for Higher Awards*, chapters 8, 16, 17 and 18.

Cross-referencing

Evidence and knowledge from this element can be used in the following mandatory units of NVQ Management Level 4: **A2**, **A4**, **C2**, **D4**; and the following optional units: **C13**, **E3**, **E5**, **E8**.

Element B3.1 Make recommendations for expenditure

Performance Criterion

(g) *You present your recommendations to relevant people in an appropriate format and at an appropriate time.*

> You will need to explain how recommendations were presented to show them in the most appropriate way. Explain who the people were and their relevance. They should include at least two of the following: team members, peers, senior employees and financial specialists.

Interpretation

▪ How were your recommendations presented?

▪ Who were the relevant people?

▪ How did you ensure that the format used presented your recommendations in the clearest possible way?

Candidate illustration

Event route
Val followed organisational procedures and forwarded her report to her manager. It was then considered by senior managers and the finance section. She explained her compliance with procedures in a personal statement and included correspondence with the finance section requesting a meeting with her to discuss specific parts of the report. The minutes of the meeting were also included as evidence.

Event route
Kieron distributed a written financial report relating to export strategies to the director and other managers on his level. He then gave a verbal presentation justifying his strategy and explaining why alternatives had not been considered. He cross-referenced to his report from previous performance criteria within this element and included samples of overhead transparencies used during the presentation. He also submitted a witness testimony from the director explaining that other managers were present, as the strategy would impact on their role and targets for future performance.

Ideas for evidence

▪ Financial reports.

▪ Correspondence with relevant people.

▪ Details of presentations given.

▪ Personal statement and witness testimony explaining who relevant people were.

Your ideas for evidence

Description of evidence	Location of evidence	Opportunities for cross-referencing	Reflection and analysis

K&U links

Suggested reading for knowledge and understanding purposes:

Cole, G.A., *Management: Theory and Practice*, 5th edition, chapters 19 and 52.

Mullins, L.J., *Management and Organisational Behaviour*, 4th edition, chapter 17.

Needham, D. et al., *Business for Higher Awards*, chapters 8, 16, 17 and 18.

Cross-referencing

Evidence and knowledge from this element can be used in the following mandatory units of NVQ Management Level 4: **A2, A4, C2, D4**; and the following optional units: **C13, E3, E5, E8**.

| *Element* B3.2 | **Control expenditure against budgets** |

Performance Criterion

(a) *You give team members clear and consistent advice on how they can help to control expenditure.*

> To meet the requirements of this PC you should focus on specific instances where you have involved staff in monitoring and controlling expenditure. Explain the circumstances and the nature of the advice provided.

Interpretation

▉ When have you given this kind of advice to members of your team?

▉ Why have you given this advice?

▉ How have you ensured that the advice you have given is clear and consistent?

Candidate illustration

Event route
Val was able to cross-reference to Element B3.1, PC (a), in which she distributed the standardised budgeting document and explained her requirements at a meeting. She explained about the pro-forma and how it had been designed to assist team members in budgeting for and controlling expenditure.

Kieron included evidence relating to his national sales team's expense accounts. These accounts consisted mainly of costs relating to travel, vehicle maintenance, communications and subsistence. Kieron routinely provided advice to sales people regarding expenses and how to keep them to a minimum. In response to a recent increase in mobile phone calls and petrol costs, Kieron called a meeting with the sales team and provided guidelines on how to minimise mobile phone use and petrol consumption. Kieron included the guidelines and minutes of the meeting as evidence, and explained the circumstances in his analysis.

Ideas for evidence

▉ Minutes of meetings discussing budgetary control with team members.

▉ Paperwork designed to assist in controlling expenditure.

▉ Personal statement detailing actions taken.

▉ Witness testimony from team members involved.

Your ideas for evidence

Description of evidence	Location of evidence	Opportunities for cross-referencing	Reflection and analysis

K&U links

Suggested reading for knowledge and understanding purposes:

Cole, G.A., *Management: Theory and Practice*, 5th edition, chapters 19 and 52.

Mullins, L.J., *Management and Organisational Behaviour*, 4th edition, chapter 17.

Needham, D. et al., *Business for Higher Awards*, chapters 8, 16, 17 and 18.

Cross-referencing

Evidence and knowledge from this element can be used in the following mandatory units of NVQ Management Level 4: **A2**, **A4**, **C2**, **D4**; and the following optional units: **C13**, **E3**, **E5**, **E8**.

Element B3.2 **Control expenditure against budgets**

Performance Criterion

(b) You give team members opportunities to take individual responsibility for monitoring and controlling expenditure.

Highlight instances where you have given individual members of your team specific responsibility for monitoring and controlling areas of expenditure. Expenditure should concern two of the following areas: supplies, people, overhead expenses and capital equipment.

Interpretation

■ To which team members have you given this kind of responsibility?

■ Why were they the appropriate people?

■ How were opportunities provided?

Candidate illustration

Val had a memo from the finance department drawing her attention to her rising office stationery costs. She had requested one of the administrative staff to design a stock control system for stationery that could be used by the team. When this had been done, Val arranged for the member of staff to give a presentation to the rest of the team to explain it. The team recorded all stationery used and stock numbers were monitored by staff. The system was used as evidence, together with Val's initial request for the work to be undertaken.

Kieron routinely gave members of his sales team responsibility for monitoring their expenditure through record keeping and the submission of receipts. Examples of these and witness testimony from two sales staff were included as evidence.

Ideas for evidence

■ Products of team members' monitoring expenditure:
  – records;
  – receipts.

■ Notes of briefing sessions held with staff.

■ Witness testimony from staff involved.

Your ideas for evidence

Description of evidence	Location of evidence	Opportunities for cross-referencing	Reflection and analysis

K&U links   Suggested reading for knowledge and understanding purposes:

Cole, G.A., *Management: Theory and Practice,* 5th edition, chapters 19 and 52.

Mullins, L.J., *Management and Organisational Behaviour,* 4th edition, chapter 17.

Needham, D. et al., *Business for Higher Awards,* chapters 8, 16, 17 and 18.

Cross-referencing   Evidence and knowledge from this element can be used in the following mandatory units of NVQ Management Level 4: **A2, A4, C2, D4**; and the following optional units: **C13, E3, E5, E8.**

Element B3.2	**Control expenditure against budgets**

Performance Criterion

(c) *Your methods of monitoring expenditure are reliable and comply with organisational requirements.*

> You will have to explain your methods of monitoring expenditure. Include at least two of the following methods: considering oral information; considering written information; and by examining financial information. Explain any organisational procedures and requirements that impact on your methods of monitoring.

Interpretation

- Which methods of monitoring expenditure against budgets do you use?
- How do you ensure that your methods are reliable?

Candidate illustration

Kieron was able to cross-reference to the methods used by staff to monitor expenditure. Individual staff members' records were used by Kieron to provide monthly expenditure reports, using computer-based systems operated across the organisation. Kieron invited his NVQ assessor to observe this computerised system in order to maintain confidentiality requirements. He was observed compiling an expenditure report and answered several questions from his assessor. The assessor's report on the observation, together with a written record of the questions and answers, was submitted as evidence.

Val submitted her own paper-based records of the team's expenditure and explained the organisational requirements and standardised systems for monitoring and reporting used.

Ideas for evidence

- Cross-reference to evidence used for this unit, if appropriate.
- Records of monitoring expenditure that illustrate methods.
- Personal statement explaining organisational requirements.
- Records of observations and questioning carried out by your NVQ advisor or assessor.

Your ideas for evidence

Description of evidence	Location of evidence	Opportunities for cross-referencing	Reflection and analysis

K&U links

Suggested reading for knowledge and understanding purposes:

Cole, G.A., *Management: Theory and Practice,* 5th edition, chapters 19 and 52.

Mullins, L.J., *Management and Organisational Behaviour,* 4th edition, chapter 17.

Needham, D. et al., *Business for Higher Awards,* chapters 8, 16, 17 and 18.

Cross-referencing

Evidence and knowledge from this element can be used in the following mandatory units of NVQ Management Level 4: **A2, A4,**

Element B3.2 Control expenditure against budgets

Performance Criterion

(d) You monitor expenditure against agreed budgets at appropriate intervals.

> Detail specific instances and examples of areas that you have monitored. At least two of the following types of expenditure must be included: supplies, people, overhead expenses and capital equipment. Focus on timescales involved and explain why they are significant.

Interpretation

▌ How do you monitor expenditure?

▌ What areas of expenditure are monitored?

▌ What timescales are involved?

Candidate illustration

Event route
Val continued her focus on stationery expenditure (see PC (b)). To ensure that expenditure was within budgets, she monitored expenditure monthly. Notes of Val's monitoring and records were submitted as evidence, together with a testimony from her manager confirming her actions.

Event route
Kieron also cross-referenced to his monitoring of sales staff's expenses (see PC (a)) through their weekly submission of individual records and receipts. His collation of this information, and a personal statement explaining the timescales involved, were submitted as evidence.

Ideas for evidence

▌ Cross-reference to evidence used for this unit, if appropriate.

▌ Products of your monitoring of expenditure:
  – records;
  – notes;
  – computerised printouts.

▌ Personal statement explaining the appropriateness of the timescales involved.

Your ideas for evidence

Description of evidence	Location of evidence	Opportunities for cross-referencing	Reflection and analysis

K&U links

Suggested reading for knowledge and understanding purposes:

Cole, G.A., *Management: Theory and Practice,* 5th edition, chapters 19 and 52.

Mullins, L.J., *Management and Organisational Behaviour,* 4th edition, chapter 17.

Needham, D. et al., *Business for Higher Awards,* chapters 8, 16, 17 and 18.

Cross-referencing

Evidence and knowledge from this element can be used in the following mandatory units of NVQ Management Level 4: **A2, A4, C2, D4**; and the following optional units: **C13, E3, E5, E8.**

Element B3.2 Control expenditure against budgets

Performance Criterion

(e) *You control expenditure in line with budgets and organisational requirements.*

> You can link to previous performance criteria within this element, if relevant. Explain how expenditure is controlled. Illustrate your compliance by using specific examples and providing background information to put the evidence into context. Again, explain any organisational requirements and how you comply with them.

Interpretation

▮ What actions do you take to control expenditure?

▮ How do you ensure that control is in line with allocated budgets?

▮ Which organisational requirements impact on the control of expenditure?

Candidate illustration

Event route
In monitoring stationery expenditure within the office, Val was able to set limits on the numbers of items that could be issued to individual members of staff. These were communicated by memo to all members of staff. The memo and cross-references to the system employed (see PC (b)) were submitted as evidence, as well as the office stationery budget and a memo from the finance office which asked departments to reduce expenditure in this area.

Event route
Kieron was able to cross-reference to his monitoring of sales staff's expense claims (see PC (a)). In addition, Kieron controlled this expenditure through comparisons with projected amounts allocated to expense claims. The observations and questioning carried out by Kieron's NVQ assessor also covered the requirements of this performance criterion.

Ideas for evidence

▮ Cross-reference to evidence used for this unit, if appropriate.

▮ Products of your controlling of expenditure:
  – records;
  – notes;
  – memos and correspondence;
  – computerised printouts.

▮ Records of observations and questioning carried out by your NVQ advisor or assessor.

▮ Personal statement detailing organisational context and actions taken.

▮ Witness testimony from those involved.

Your ideas for evidence

Description of evidence	Location of evidence	Opportunities for cross-referencing	Reflection and analysis

K&U links

Suggested reading for knowledge and understanding purposes:

Cole, G.A., *Management: Theory and Practice,* 5th edition, chapters 19 and 52.

Mullins, L.J., *Management and Organisational Behaviour,* 4th edition, chapter 17.

Needham, D. et al., *Business for Higher Awards,* chapters 8, 16, 17 and 18.

Cross-referencing

Evidence and knowledge from this element can be used in the following mandatory units of NVQ Management Level 4: **A2, A4, C2, D4**; and the following optional units: **C13, E3, E5, E8**.

Element B3.2   Control expenditure against budgets

Performance Criterion

(f) *The corrective action you take in response to actual or potential significant variations from budget is prompt and complies with organisational requirements.*

> You should identify a specific instance where you have had to take corrective action. Detail the organisational context and the likely implications of the variation from budget. Your evidence should contain at least two examples of the following corrective actions: altering activities; rescheduling expenditure; altering budget allocations within the limits of your responsibility; and negotiating budgets.

Interpretation

▉ Under what circumstances have you had to take corrective action in response to actual or potential variations from budget?

▉ What actions were taken?

▉ What were the timescales involved and why were these appropriate?

▉ Which organisational requirements were relevant?

Candidate illustration

Event route
Val was able to cross-reference to all the evidence used previously in this element concerning stationery expenditure (beginning at PC (b)), as it clearly detailed actions taken in response to overspending on stationery. Val's actions were also clearly explained in the analysis of her evidence.

Event route
Kieron focused on the employment of part-time temporary sales staff on a commission-only basis. He identified that part-time sales figures for one month did not warrant the associated employment costs, as a result of which one contract was not renewed. Kieron detailed his analysis of figures in a personal report, including a printout of the figures on which the decisions were taken. Kieron also had to seek authority to act from his manager, the director. The memo and reply detailing the corrective action proposed were also evidenced.

Ideas for evidence

▉ Cross-reference to evidence used for this unit, if appropriate.

▉ Products of corrective action taken:
– changes in actions;
– rescheduling of expenditure;
– altering of budgetary allocations.

▉ Personal statement explaining actions taken.

▉ Correspondence detailing proposed corrective action.

▉ Witness testimony from others involved.

Your ideas for evidence

Description of evidence	Location of evidence	Opportunities for cross-referencing	Reflection and analysis

K&U links

Suggested reading for knowledge and understanding purposes:

Cole, G.A., *Management: Theory and Practice*, 5th edition, chapters 19 and 52.

Mullins, L.J., *Management and Organisational Behaviour*, 4th edition, chapter 17.

Needham, D. et al., *Business for Higher Awards*, chapters 8, 16, 17 and 18.

Cross-referencing

Evidence and knowledge from this element can be used in the following mandatory units of NVQ Management Level 4: **A2, A4,**

Control expenditure against budgets

Performance Criterion

(g) *You refer requests for expenditure outside your responsibility promptly to the appropriate people.*

> You will find it helpful if you explain your span of control and authority regarding expenditure. Detail specific instances where you have referred requests for expenditure and explain the circumstances. Highlight why you referred requests to particular people within your organisation.

Interpretation

- Under what circumstances have you had to refer requests for expenditure to others?
- What was the nature of the request?
- What were the timescales involved?
- Who were the appropriate people?

Candidate illustration

Val included a personal statement detailing the limits of her authority concerning expenditure. She detailed an incident when the team, during a weekly review meeting, requested the purchase of a pager to facilitate communication for staff who were constantly out of the office. As Val did not have a budget heading for such expenditure the request was referred to the finance section through her line manager by email. The request was supported by a report justifying the expenditure. This report was also included as evidence, alongside the email printout which showed the date of the request and a photocopy of her diary showing the date the review meeting was held.

Kieron received a request from a member of his team for funding to attend a sales conference. In accordance with company policy, Kieron referred the request to the director. Kieron did not support the request and gave his reasons in a note forwarded to the director with the request. This note, together with the request and correspondence with the director, was submitted as evidence.

Ideas for evidence

- Correspondence concerning requests for expenditure.
- Personal statement explaining your limits of authority concerning expenditure.
- Reports justifying expenditure.

Your ideas for evidence

Description of evidence	Location of evidence	Opportunities for cross-referencing	Reflection and analysis

K&U links

Suggested reading for knowledge and understanding purposes:

Cole, G.A., *Management: Theory and Practice*, 5th edition, chapters 19 and 52.

Mullins, L.J., *Management and Organisational Behaviour*, 4th edition, chapter 17.

Needham, D. et al., *Business for Higher Awards*, chapters 8, 16, 17 and 18.

Cross-referencing

Evidence and knowledge from this element can be used in the following mandatory units of NVQ Management Level 4: **A2**, **A4**, **C2**, **D4**; and the following optional units: **C13**, **E3**, **E5**, **E8**.

| *Element B3.2* | **Control expenditure against budgets** |

Performance Criterion

(h) *Your records of expenditure are complete, accurate and available to authorised people only.*

> You should link to previous performance criteria from this element, if appropriate. Explain your recording system and the provisions that are made to ensure accuracy and confidentiality.

Interpretation

▌ What financial records are kept?

▌ How are they maintained?

▌ How is confidentiality assured?

Candidate illustration

Event route
Both Kieron and Val cross-referenced to existing evidence used for this element. Val also included a witness testimony from her line manager confirming the accuracy of her record keeping and her adherence to confidentiality guidelines.

Ideas for evidence

▌ Cross-reference to records already included as evidence for this element.

▌ Witness testimony from others involved.

▌ Records of observation and questioning from your NVQ advisor or assessor.

▌ Personal statement explaining record systems.

▌ Computerised printouts of records.

Your ideas for evidence

Description of evidence	Location of evidence	Opportunities for cross-referencing	Reflection and analysis

K&U links

Suggested reading for knowledge and understanding purposes:

Cole, G.A., *Management: Theory and Practice,* 5th edition, chapters 19 and 52.

Mullins, L.J., *Management and Organisational Behaviour,* 4th edition, chapter 17.

Needham, D. et al., *Business for Higher Awards,* chapters 8, 16, 17 and 18.

Cross-referencing

Evidence and knowledge from this element can be used in the following mandatory units of NVQ Management Level 4: **A2**, **A4**, **C2**, **D4**; and the following optional units: **C13**, **E3**, **E5**, **E8**.

Glossary

Accredited Prior Learning/Achievement (APL/A) The formal recognition of your existing achievement, knowledge and/or skills.

Advice Formal support given to you by your advisor to help you achieve your NVQ.

Advisor The person allocated to help you achieve the requirements of the NVQ.

Assessment The process undertaken by the assessor of comparing the evidence you put forward with the NVQ standards in order to determine whether you are competent in that area.

Assessment centre The organisation responsible for the process of assessment, including quality assurance and the appointment and management of suitable assessors. These have to be approved by the awarding body.

Assessment decisions The formal decision made by your assessor. These take three forms: competent, not yet competent and insufficient evidence.

Assessors The people appointed by the assessment centre to judge your evidence against the NVQ standards.

Awarding body A body recognised by the lead body and responsible for 'packaging' NVQ standards into qualifications that can be awarded to candidates. There are currently 16 awarding bodies for the NVQ in Management at Level 4.

Candidate An individual who has registered with an awarding body and who has begun to develop a portfolio of evidence (i.e. you!).

Candidate questioning The process of generating evidence whereby the assessor or advisor will ask you questions and make a formal record of the process.

Competence The ability to perform your job to the nationally recognised standard.

Competent An assessment decision which confirms that your evidence meets the nationally recognised standards.

Elements of competence The description of a specific aspect of performance associated with a particular work activity.

Evidence Anything which is put forward in order to show competence within the NVQ framework.

Evidence collection The process of gathering evidence to put forward for assessment.

External verification Part of the quality assurance process, undertaken by the awarding body, which ensures that the assessment of candidates meets its requirements.

Insufficient evidence An assessment decision which means that you could not be assessed 'competent' because of a lack of evidence.

Internal verification Part of the quality assurance process, undertaken by the assessment centre, which ensures that the assessment process meets the standards of the awarding body.

Knowledge and understanding (K&U) The theoretical and underpinning knowledge relevant to your job.

Lead body An organisation responsible for identifying the nationally acceptable standards of performance relevant to a particular industry. The lead body for the Management NVQs is the Management Charter Initiative (MCI).

Level The NVQ level reflects the amount of competence, knowledge, initiative, responsibility and autonomy associated with each stage in the NVQ framework. There are five levels of NVQ.

Management Charter Initiative (MCI) The lead body for the Management NVQs. Through consultation they have developed the management standards and are responsible for their upkeep.

Mandatory units The core or mandatory units of the NVQ reflect those activities that would normally be undertaken by all managers at a specific level of management. There are six mandatory units in the Management NVQ at Level 4.

National Council for Vocational Qualifications (NCVQ) Please see Qualifications and Curriculum Authority (QCA).

National Vocational Qualifications (NVQs) These are qualifications based on nationally recognised occupational standards which prescribe the expected standard of performance in a job.

Naturally occurring evidence This is evidence that occurs as a result of an activity in which you are already involved or will be undertaking as part of your normal working routine (usually termed 'performance evidence').

Not yet competent The assessment decision given when you have not proved your competence.

Observation The method of assessing evidence which relies on you demonstrating your competence in front of the assessor.

Observational analysis sheet A written record of the assessment process when it has been undertaken through observation.

Optional units The optional units of the NVQ allow you to select those that most closely reflect your areas of management responsibility. You should select three optional units from a choice of 18 in the Management NVQ at Level 4.

Performance criterion (PC) The specific behaviour or outcome associated with an element of competence. These are the standards against which you are assessed.

Performance evidence Evidence that has occurred naturally as a result of your job (sometimes termed 'naturally occurring evidence').

Personal statements Accounts by candidates detailing work performance. They are often needed in order to contextualise performance evidence, i.e. to provide the assessor with some background or other necessary additional information or explanation.

Portfolio Your compilation of evidence used to demonstrate competence.

Qualifications and Curriculum Authority (QCA) The organisation responsible for overseeing all NVQs in the UK outside Scotland. It was formed in 1997, bringing together the National Council for Vocational Qualifications (NCVQ) and the School Curriculum and Assessment Authority (SCAA). The QCA formally recognises NVQs and audits the activity of awarding bodies.

Random sampling The process of choosing a sample of portfolios to be verified for quality assurance purposes.

Reflection and analysis The process of explanation you undertake to clarify why the evidence put forward meets the standards of competence stipulated by the NVQ.

Registration The process of signing up with an awarding body.

Scottish Qualifications Authority (SQA) The organisation responsible for overseeing all NVQs in Scotland. The SCA formally recognises SVQs and audits the activity of awarding bodies.

Scottish Vocational Qualification (SVQ) The Scottish equivalent of National Vocational Qualifications (NVQs).

Simulated training activities Any training or development opportunity outside the candidate's normal job which is undertaken purely to meet the requirements of the NVQ.

Standards The lead body's description of competence for a specific job.

Supplementary evidence Evidence that is put forward in addition to performance evidence. This is often in the form of personal statements or testimonies.

Units of competence A group of standards that reflect a specific area of a job.

Vocational education and training Education and training based on candidates' performance in their job, not in the classroom. Vocational qualifications 'focus on your performance at work, how you use your skills, apply your knowledge and the available resources to achieve results' (MCI, 1997).

Witness testimonies Statements made by others as to your performance in the workplace.

Bibliography

Beaumont, G., 1997, *Review of 100 NVQs and SVQs*, A Report Submitted to the Department for Education and Employment.

Cole, G.A., 1996, *Management: Theory and Practice*, 5th edition, Letts Educational, London.

Constable and McCormick, 1987, *The Making of British Managers*, BIM/CBI.

Dakers, H., 1996, *NVQs and How to Get Them*, Kogan Page.

Department for Education and Employment, 1996, 'The Specification of Knowledge and Understanding for NVQs and SVQs: Six Case Studies', *Competence and Assessment Briefing Series*, 11.

Fletcher, S., 1992, *Competence-Based Assessment Techniques*, Kogan Page.

Handy, C., Gow and Moloney, 1987, *The Making of Managers*, NDEC/MSC/BIM.

Jessup, G., 1991, *Outcomes: NVQs and the Emerging Model of Education and Training*, Falmer Press.

Longworth, N. and Davies, W.K., 1996, *Lifelong Learning*, Kogan Page.

Management Charter Initiative (MCI), 1997, *What are Management Qualifications? An Introduction*.

Mullins, L.J., 1996, *Management and Organisational Behaviour*, 4th edition, Pitman Publishing, London.

Needham, D., Dransfield, R., Harris, R. and Coles, M., 1995, *Business for Higher Awards*, Heinemann, Oxford.

Qualifications and Curriculum Authority, 1997, *DataNews*, Issue 6, Winter.

Example of completed reflection and analysis documentation

ANALYSIS OF EVIDENCE.

Name: Val XXX

NVQ LEVEL 3/4 – SUPERVISORY MANAGEMENT/MANAGEMENT STANDARDS.

(delete as applicable)

EL.	PERF. CRIT.	ANALYSIS and REFLECTION	EVID. REF.	AGREED (ASS'OR)
C2.1	(a)	I have included copies of my self-appraisal documentation. The first one I have included (EV1) was completed in September last year and the second one (EV2) was filled out in January of this year. As part of the self-appraisal process we have to identify our development goals for the coming quarter and then develop an action plan which will enable us to meet those goals. As you will see the action plan also requires us to set deadlines for each activity. It is a requirement of the self-appraisal process to monitor the achievement of these goals and activities against the deadlines set.	EV1 and EV2	
C2.1	(b)	Self-appraisal is not the only way that development needs are identified within my organisation. This is also done through consultation with my line manager during appraisal and supervision sessions. I have included some extracts from these records which demonstrate how my manager has helped me identify current development objectives (EV3) and future objectives (EV4). One future development need was identified as a result of compiling our annual management team's business plan (EV5). In order to meet our legal obligations an improved database was needed in order to store client records in a way that met current legislative requirements. In order to manage this database and support my staff I would need some training on the system. This request was made to my line manager during a supervision session (EV4).	EV3 and EV4 and EV5	

Please use additional sheets as required.

Example of completed assessor's feedback sheet

Assessor Feedback Sheet	Unit Number D1	Element 3

NVQ Level 2~~~~3~~ 4 ~~5~~

Name of Candidate `Val XXX`   Name of Assessor `Cathy Parker`

Period of Evidence   From: September 1997   To: January 1998

Type of Evidence (tick as appropriate)

WORK BASED		TRAINING		OTHER	
Own original work	√	Project		Voluntary work	
Product of work	√	Assignment			
Personal report		Exercise(s)			
Diary/Logbook		Case-study			
Witness Testimony		Simulation			

Direct observation: Yes ☐   No ☑

Oral questioning necessary: Yes ☐   No ☑

Feedback

PC	Feedback	Summary of action to be taken	Assessment decision Competent Insufficient evidence Not yet competent
(a)	Your self-appraisal documentation clearly meets the requirements of this PC.	None	Competent
(b)	Although your self-appraisals detail current and future development objectives, with the exception of further training on the proposed new database system, you do not explain where these objectives have come from.	Please write a short personal statement which explains why the development objectives in your self-appraisal/action plan are included. What has led you to include them as development objectives? How have you prioritised these in your action plan?	Insufficient evidence

Feedback continued overleaf: Yes ☐   No ☐

Assessment Decision

This candidate is ~~competent~~/not yet competent in this element.

Assessor's signature: Cathy Parker   Date: 13th March 1998

Index

Other titles of interest:

How to get a Management NVQ: Level 3: Mandatory units   Johnson & Parker
October 1998   *£14.95*

How to get a Management NVQ: Level 4: Optional units   Johnson & Parker
January 1999   *£9.95*

How to get a Management NVQ: Level 3: Optional units   Johnson & Parker
March 1999   *£9.95*

Access 97 – Basic Skills	1 85805 2998	Coles & Rowley	*£6.95*
Access 97 – Further Skills	1 85805 3005	Coles & Rowley	*£6.95*
Excel 97 – Basic Skills	1 85805 219X	Muir	*£6.95*
Excel 97 – Further Skills	1 85805 2181	Muir	*£6.95*
Office 97	1 85805 2238	Hill	*£6.95*
Powerpoint 97	1 85805 3587	Coles & Rowley	*£6.95*
Word 97 – Basic Skills	1 85805 2211	Coles & Rowley	*£6.95*
Word 97 – Further Skills	1 85805 222X	Coles & Rowley	*£6.95*
Windows 98	1 85805 3781	Muir	*£6.95*

To order copies of this book, please call 01206 255678 (bookshops)
or 01206 255777 (private customers).